Teachers
Bridging Difference

D1715004

Teachers Bridging Difference

Exploring Identity with Art

MARIT DEWHURST

Harvard Education Press

Cambridge, Massachusetts

Paperback ISBN 978-1-68253-212-6
Library Edition ISBN 978-1-68253-213-3

Library of Congress Cataloging-in-Publication Data
Names: Dewhurst, Marit., author.
Title: Teachers bridging difference : exploring identity with art / Marit
   Dewhurst.
Description: Cambridge : Massachusetts : Harvard Education Press, 2018. |
   Includes bibliographical references and index.
Identifiers: LCCN 2018015009| ISBN 9781682532126 (pbk.) | ISBN 9781682532133
   (library edition)
Subjects: LCSH: Identity (Philosophical concept) in art. | Community arts
   projects. | Intercultural communication. | Communication and the arts. |
   Social justice--Study and teaching.
Classification: LCC NX180.S6 D49 2018 | DDC 700.1/03--dc23
LC record available at https://lccn.loc.gov/2018015009

Published by Harvard Education Press,
an imprint of the Harvard Education Publishing Group

Harvard Education Press
8 Story Street
Cambridge, MA 02138

Cover Design: Ciano Design
Cover Image: Christopher M. Rose
The typefaces used in this book are Minion Pro, Myriad Pro,
and Linotype Decoration Pi 2

Contents

To the artist-educator-students with whom I have been honored to learn alongside in the art education program at the City College of New York. As James Baldwin said, "We've got to be as clear-headed about human beings as possible, because we are still each other's only hope."[1]

Thank you for being that hope for me, for your students, and for each other.

Foreword

I have fond memories of learning on Appian Way in Cambridge, Massachusetts, with Marit Dewhurst. Marit and I met in 2002 while she was pursuing a master's degree in art education, and I was pursuing a doctorate. We were young, hopeful, student activists at the Harvard Graduate School of Education (HGSE), working for educational justice while completing our degrees. Marit quickly became one of my sisters in justice work at HGSE, and I continue to be inspired by her scholarship and praxis, and its implications for transforming art education, teacher education broadly, educational research that centers educator and youth voices, and social justice work in multiple learning contexts.

We are living in a moment when activism is akin to breathing for people of various marginalized communities. For teachers in various types of educational spaces working to advance cross-cultural understanding, this activism mirrors sustained, critical self-reflection about how their identity markers (e.g., race, ethnicity, gender, sexuality, religion, etc.) interact to shape the enactment of their power and privilege in learning contexts. This type of social justice work is not simply a fad but a way to sustain teachers' and students' life ways and humanity. It is soul work. We see this evidenced in recent movements such as Black Lives Matter (#BLM), Dakota Access Pipeline protests (#NODAPL), Sanctuary Campus/Sanctuary City, support for Deferred Action for Childhood Arrivals (DACA), protests against violence toward black girls and women (#SAYHERNAME), sexual assault protests (#METOO), and protests in support of gun control (#GUNCON-TROLNOW)—movements where teachers across the country have collectively challenged themselves to understand how to effectively engage young people in discussions of equity, civility, and empathy. Educator activists have been integral in all these movements, and art has been one form of their expression of critical identity work, resisting oppressive systems, and connecting across cultural differences with colleagues, students, and community members. Art is essential to the human condition because it is a natural part of each of us. Art gives us insight into history and how it informs the present and future; it allows us to experience our full range of emotions through self-creation and reflecting on the creation of others; and it bridges gaps between cultures. In this book, Dewhurst allows the reader to experience each of these outgrowths of art expression through the lenses of teachers engaged in identity work.

Dewhurst cites Gloria Anzaldúa's writing on bridges and boundaries, and how crossing a boundary unlocks critical opportunities for transformation. The same analogy can be applied to artistic expression. Like bridges, art allows for channels and linkages that signify transitioning, crossing borders, and changing perspectives. This book beautifully nuances the richness and challenges that teachers experience—convergences and divergences—when using art to better understand the multifaceted nature of their identities and how issues of power and privilege intersect with those. What this book teaches us about the "stances" we can develop through art is central to understanding how to enact critical pedagogy and cultivate cross-cultural connections in learning spaces. Readers can expect to gain an authentic and deep understanding of how these stances foster more authentic and humanizing relationships between teachers, students, and community members.

Dewhurst's discussion of the aforementioned stances easily frames for the reader how educators can utilize art to make connections at micro (personal) and macro (systems) levels to sociopolitical issues that heighten their critical consciousness. The process of consciousness raising occurs through artistic critiques of conditions of inequity and injustice in their worlds and the larger society. Preservice and in-service teachers need to embody skills for critical identity work and model those for their students. What makes this text additionally unique is that the reader not only experiences the teachers' meaning making of developing art to better understand identity, but also gains an understanding of effective strategies that can be used across multiple contexts for enacting a critical arts pedagogy as an educator. The stances that Dewhurst takes up in this text are useful not only for art educators but also for educators across educational disciplines. As a teacher educator who focuses on issues of racial and social justice in my teaching and research, I believe readers will glean the applicability of the findings presented here across a variety of teacher education program components.

This book does not simply present findings from an empirical inquiry with current and preservice teachers; it gives us ways forward for embodying culturally responsive teaching and learning and humanizing pedagogy through engagement with art.

I have three elementary-aged daughters who are growing up during challenging national and global times. This moment requires multiple modes of expression to convey how my children and other youth are experiencing and making meaning of injustice in their schools, community, state, nation, and world. I want my daughters to be taught by teachers who understand the impact of their multifaceted identities on the lives of their students and who can also empower students (like my daughters) to express their multifaceted selves orally, in writing, and *through art*. We desperately need teachers who are products of programs that have effectively prepared them to understand issues of culture, power, and difference in the classroom, critically examine systems that dehumanize students instead of affirm their identities, and build healthy and sustained relationships with culturally diverse students and communities. Further, educators and the youth they work with need to be able to lead the way in what they learn about how to express their dreams, visions, resistance, and hopes through art media. The narratives and art of the educators and preservice teachers in this book give us hope for what education (not schooling) can and should be. Alex Grey states, "When artists give form to revelation, their art can advance, deepen, and potentially transform the consciousness of their community."[1] This book allows the reader to see this happen with teachers engaged in making art about their own identities and learning to relate to people from different backgrounds, experiences, and cultural groups. It provides a way forward for all of us and practical application for the teacher education classroom, K–12 classroom, and out-of-school learning context in what have recently been bleak times. Educators, researchers, youth, and community organizers alike will glean insights that will continue to inform how they build relationships across difference to not only meet the needs of students in schools but also equip young people with the skills to cultivate the types of communities and societies in which they truly want to live.

Dorinda J. Carter Andrews, EdD
Assistant Dean, Equity Outreach Initiatives
Associate Professor of Teacher Education
Michigan State University

Preface

Of Borders and Bridges

I began this book before the 2016 presidential election laid bare the deep and long-standing divisions in our country. From racial segregation, gender discrimination, and religious prejudice to the wage, opportunity, and wealth gaps, we live in a world of divisive borders—divisions that are largely built around our very identities. Our identities—the ways we name, experience, and understand our bodies and beliefs—can be sources of great pride and shared honor. However, these same identities can also be used to pit us against each other, to create the illusion that one type of person is better than another. The walls and gaps that result from these socially constructed divisions feed inequality and injustice.

These identity-based divisions are marked by borders—the real and imagined lines that separate one person from another. Poet and scholar Gloria Anzaldúa writes, "Borders are set up to define the places that are safe and unsafe, to distinguish us from them. A border is a dividing line, a narrow strip along a steep edge."[1] In the United States, these edges appear to be growing ever steeper. Our schools and neighborhoods are increasingly segregated by race and wealth. Our social media platforms turn ever more partisan. Even our friendships tend to be with like-minded people from similar social backgrounds. The barriers between us can seem insurmountable.

For those of us in education, these borders that separate people—borders named after parts of our identities—can feel particularly significant. We might bump against them as we try to understand our students who may be racially, culturally, economically, or simply generationally different from us. We might crash into these barriers when we try to speak with a colleague about our political or religious beliefs. We might feel blocked by walls that seem to prevent us from really connecting with the communities in which we work and live. In a field where the goal is to expand understanding, these manmade borders obstruct our work. To be effective teachers, we must cultivate our capacity to examine, cross, and reimagine the social borders that separate us.

This book is about why and how we can use art to better understand our different identities—be they tied to our race, culture, class, gender, religion, sexual orientation, ability, or nationality. It is about using art to investigate the personal and structural ways in which power and privilege intersect with our identities to affect how we relate to one another. And, at its hopeful core, this book is about how the arts can provide educators and their students with tools to connect with people across the borders that too often divide us. As many educators know, the ability to understand our students, their families, and their communities is imperative if we aim to facilitate empowering learning experiences. Educator Paulo Freire writes, "Educators need to know what happens in the world of the children with whom they will work. They need to know the universe of their dreams, the language with which they skillfully defend themselves from the aggressiveness of their world, what they know independently of the school, and how they know it."[2] The question is, how do we do this? What does it take to find our way across these borders to really understand the universes within each of us?

Writing of bridges, Anzaldúa describes how the act of crossing a boundary unlocks critical opportunities for transformation:

> Bridges are thresholds to other realities, archetypal, primal symbols of shifting consciousness. They are passageways, conduits, and connectors that connote transitioning, crossing borders, and changing perspectives. Bridges span liminal (threshold) spaces between worlds, spaces I call *nepantla*, a Nahuatl word meaning *tierra entre medio*. Transformations occur in this in-between space, an unstable, unpredictable, precarious, always-in-transition space lacking clear boundaries."[3]

Bridges—as overused as the metaphor might be—still offer us the clearest visual for the kind of opening that can happen when we connect across a border. Suddenly, the steep edges can appear less daunting and the distance apart less impassable. While I am not so naive to believe that simply nurturing metaphorical bridges across the social divisions in our country will radically alter the inequality that pervades, I do believe that those of us in education must find ways to teach and learn across the barriers that society has built between us. Without a concerted effort to connect with people whose identities we have been taught to see as distant, the borders and divisions between us will certainly widen.

Introduction

Stances for Bridging Difference

We have to restore the neighbor to the hood.[1]

—Grace Lee Boggs

As a child, I was often instructed to sit quietly whenever my folklorist-parents' tape recorder flashed red, a sign that they were deep in conversation with a traditional artist. At Native American powwows, through Northern Thai craft markets, and in South African living rooms, I sat quietly listening. Immersed in their conversations, I listened as porcupine quill box makers and beading craftswomen told stories about how making art allowed them to communicate cultural values and to reveal community histories. In overheard conversations, I learned how African American step-dancing teams cultivated a sense of community and critiqued dominant historical narratives. Among NAMES Project quilters, I heard how making a quilt to memorialize someone's life was an act of resistance, advocacy, and freedom. In kitchens, church basements, backyards, and community festivals, always through the lens of various art forms, I learned of lives much different from my own.

As a young adult, I taught theater, visual art, and poetry in community centers, youth detention centers, and afterschool programs. Working with communities of people with whom I thought I had little in common, I marveled at the ways in which we could address our shared and very different identities through making art together. Tasked with the challenge to create something collaboratively, we asked questions of each other that we wouldn't typically ask, were we to meet elsewhere: What do you believe in? What are you scared of? What separates us? Making art, it seemed, offered us a chance to dive into the meaty issues of life. And with each encounter, I learned something new about someone else's perspective of the world—and my own. I often left these encounters wondering what would be revealed next.

As a researcher and student, I began to compare my experiences with the arts in various communities with theories of learning, community development, sociology, critical pedagogy, and art education. Through countless maps and memos, qualitative studies, and reflective writing, I started to see an interconnected landscape of ideas. I looked through critical lenses that helped me see how factors of power and privilege shape this landscape. Slowly, a contextualized understanding of my world—and the worlds of my students—came into focus. With an eye toward researching the potential of the arts as a space for cross-cultural learning, I began to see connections to the practices of the arts and the educational theories I studied.

These days, I find myself in the role of educator and director of an art education program—tasked with preparing artists and educators to teach in schools, community organizations, and museums. While there is certainly much to learn about curriculum design, assessment, human development, and reflective practice, none of this will matter if educators cannot connect with their students. In a society where we struggle to relate to people who are somehow different from us, I've come to see that perhaps one of the most important skills I can nurture in my students is their capacity to know themselves, their students, and the ways in which our lives intersect across sociocultural differences. This is made even more necessary when the overwhelming majority of teachers in the United States are white, while young people under the age of eighteen are now predominantly people who do not identify as white.[2] Given these statistics, it is a rather safe assumption that teachers and students are often meeting each other across racial, cultural, ethnic, and gender differences. In an ideal world, this might not matter; however, as author and professor Christopher Emdin points out, "The reality is that we privilege people who look and act like us, and perceive those who don't as different and, frequently, inferior."[3] We can do better. Now, more than ever, when a climate crisis looms, political divisions render friendships silent, and the social networks that have often linked us together unravel, we need each other. As educators, our responsibility is to do better—to learn how to navigate our different identities with critical awareness, empathy, and humanity and to help our students learn how to connect with people across real and perceived differences. If we can't do this, I (like many others) fear our shared future.

ABOUT THE BOOK

This book argues that the arts can play a central role—one that has long been overlooked by many in the field—in helping us develop the skills, attitudes, and strategies necessary to better understand how our identities shape who we are and how we move in the world. Drawing on the findings from my research as well as my own teaching experience, this book blends scholarship from multiple disciplines with empirical research to offer a set of arts-based *stances* focused on deepening our understanding of our multiple identities. Along the way, I'll introduce many of the students who have taken my course "Identity, Community, and Culture in Art Education" at the City College of New York and are now using art to teach and learn about identity in their own in classrooms, museums, and community organizations.[4]

Following a similar trajectory as the course, each chapter will introduce a generative *stance* to cultivate to better understand how identity shapes our lives and connections with others. Within these stances, I will highlight two arts activities that can help us *turn inward* to reflect on our own biases and assumptions as well as on how they can enable us to *lean outward* to learn about other people's experience of the world. Designed to be accessible to those with little arts experience, the creative activities rely heavily on observation, research, interaction, and reflection as the basis for creating (mostly) visual art. The example activities can be used by both educators seeking to deepen their own understandings and with younger learners to build critical understanding and community within the classroom and beyond. Teacher educators and education administrators in schools and beyond will find these activities useful in courses and professional development workshops on building community, nurturing multicultural education, and identity awareness. While the book offers a suggestion for moving through each of the stances in a scaffolded order, each chapter can stand alone for readers who are interested in focusing their attention on one area of growth. The appendixes provide additional information on relevant artists and related readings to extend the ideas offered here. Moving beyond the notion of the arts as merely an illustrative medium to express emotions or as simple warm-up activities for nurturing teamwork, this book highlights how looking at and making art serve as complex tools for deepening our understandings of ourselves, our students, and the communities we aim to nurture.

SCHOLARSHIP AND FRAMEWORKS

The work of navigating the borders and bridges of identity is not new territory; artists, scholars, educators, poets, performers, and community organizers have much to teach us about how to learn and teach about identity. Much like the teaching that motivated this book, the theoretical foundation relies on several intersecting bodies of literature. Inspired by traditions of community organizing, folklore studies, intergroup dialogues, and culturally responsive and multicultural education, this book builds on existing scholarship to add an additional arts-focused layer to the conversation. Founded on my belief in the importance of talking *about* and building *across* identity divisions as a critical first step in any justice-oriented education, I have drawn knowledge and perspectives from the following bodies of scholarship.

From *community and cultural organizing* scholarship, I draw on the importance of and strategies for cross-cultural coalition building, and culture as a source of knowledge and power.[5] Community organizers prioritize the often undervalued but ultimately imperative work of building relationships between and among groups of people as they seek to shift systemic power. They value the personal stories and connections between people both as tools for individual growth and as sources for social and cultural capital. They have much to teach us about what it takes to listen closely to people, to persist in the tough work of navigating difference and conflict, and to nurture truly multifaceted communities of people.

With roots in understanding cultural production and community knowledge, I turn to *folklore studies* for theories about the artist as a critical agent in upholding community values and traditions as well as practical suggestions for fieldwork that is sensitive to relational learning.[6] Folklorists know the value of cultural production as it has long been used to cultivate community, share value systems, innovate within changing social landscapes, and promote a sense of connectedness. Describing this field, folklorist Barbara Kirschenblatt-Gimblett writes, "Basket making, traditional singing, storytelling, wit and humor in conversation, needlework, cooking, games, and pastimes—these skills are learned in the academies of the street, home, the park, the woods. And the masters are the people rooted in community and history. They acquire their skills for the most part informally from others, and with those skills they acquire deeply felt values, standards of excellence, and a resonant sense of who they are and where they are."[7] Those who study these traditions understand what it means to research the living and dynamic cultural contexts in which artists work. Folklore studies help us see the everyday art making that happens all around us for what it is: a source of vital human expression and social activity.

Within the rich scholarship on *multicultural education* and its more recent companion, *culturally responsive education*, there is significant research to explain why any effort to teach and learn about identity must address how power and privilege shape our own identities, our relationships with others, and our interactions with institutions.[8] Born of the idea that education should be inclusive of all identities, multicultural education has been at times critiqued for how it is often invoked in surface-level discussions of identity. These "food and festivals" approaches serve only to draw attention to some of the basic features of who we are, without delving deeper into the social dimensions of our relationships within and across our various identities. However, these versions of multicultural education lack the depth that many scholars advise. To maintain the focus on equity, some scholars have recently shifted the conversation toward "culturally responsive education." In their extensive writing on the subject, scholars Ana María Villegas and Tamara Lucas describe six key characteristics of the culturally responsive educator:

> Such a teacher (a) is socioculturally conscious, that is, recognizes that there are multiple ways of perceiving reality and that these ways are influenced by one's location in the social order; (b) has affirming views of students from diverse backgrounds, seeing resources for learning in all students rather than viewing differences as problems to be overcome; (c) sees himself or herself as both responsible for and capable of bringing about educational change that will make schools more responsive to all students; (d) understands how learners construct knowledge and is capable of promoting learners' knowledge construction; (e) knows about the lives of his or her students; and (f) uses his or her knowledge about students' lives to design instruction that builds on what they already know while stretching them beyond the familiar.[9]

This advice underscores the importance of knowing and valuing the full complexity of identity.

Finally, in *social justice art education*, we see how art can be a useful tool for critiquing and creating art about identity as a social and political tool.[10] Scholarship in this domain suggests that, when paired with social justice principles, the process of making and discussing works of art can foster critical reflection and activism. Artists working in this realm create works of art that shed light on oft-neglected narratives, analyze factors of inequality, and help audiences reimagine new ways of being in the world. Through their artwork, they can prompt individual development and encourage community and social engagement. Connecting to the disciplines I've highlighted, social justice art education suggests that art should not be overlooked as a vehicle for teaching and learning about identity.

WHY ART?

Standing on a ladder, artist Ana Teresa Fernández paints the border fence between Mexico and the United States a shade of sky blue that causes each painted section to seemingly disappear. St. Louis–based artist Damon Davis pastes giant images of the multiracial hands of Black Lives Matter protestors on boarded-up windows. Empower, a group of young LGBTQ and ally artists in Toronto, posts a series of web videos teaching other youth how to "do burlesque and drag."[11] Every day, artists invite us to engage with our multiple and intersecting identities. This is nothing new. Throughout human history, the arts—visual and/or performance-based—have given people tools for narrating, shaping, and making meaning of their experiences in the world.[12] As arts educator Graeme Chalmers writes, "[A]ll groups need and use art for purposes of identity, continuity, and change and to enhance their cultural values."[13] People in every culture across time and place have employed the arts to document, convey, and communicate ideas about who we are and how we can relate to each other.[14] Given this history, the arts offer educators an ideal tool for learning how to build relationships across the borders of our many identities.

The making of art, like the making of identity, is both a personal and social endeavor. Artist Yong Soon Min describes this process in her artwork: "Art making for me is a process of discovery and learning about myself and my relationship to the world. This art making also involves my desire to communicate and to share this exploration and understanding with others and thereby complete the dynamic."[15] Making art about what we value and how we experience the world offers opportunities for critical reflection about *why* we are who we are. Delving into these questions about the relationships we have with each other requires a certain comfort with complexity, ambiguity, vulnerability, and inquiry—all skills that many artists speak of in their work. As part of my research for this book, I asked every educator I interviewed why they thought that art offered such a potent space for learning and teaching about identity. Their responses, many of which I include here in full and weave throughout the following chapters, speak eloquently about their decisions to use art to teach and learn about identity in their classrooms.

Art Gives Us Glimpses of Our Students

This opportunity to learn about ourselves, each other, and the ways our identities intersect, overlap, and surprise us can give educators a tool to better understand the inner lives of their students. Andy, a former student of mine who is now a teacher in a high school for those who are older than conventionally aged students, described a recent art project he completed with students that allowed him to gain a more nuanced insight into one of his students. When one student used imagery that referenced her Haitian heritage, Andy noted that "it was the only time in several years of knowing her that she shared about her Haitian heritage." Through her artwork, Andy came to know another facet of his student's identity.

Art Helps Students See Themselves

In talking about why she uses conversations about artworks as a teaching tool, Shannon, a museum educator and former student in my course, pointed to how in "the art, you get to build and understand in different ways which relates to your identity because you're constantly changing." Shannon draws our attention to an important element of making art about oneself—who we are is in a constant state of flux based on context, our own growth, and who we are with. Therefore, when we make art about ourselves, it can serve as both a mirror to our current experiences and a record of who we have been over time. Describing this, Jackie, an artist, museum educator, and former student of mine, noted how creating art can provide learners with a way to see themselves in new ways: "We need an object outside of ourselves. So that we can look at ourselves, like taking yourself and putting it into an artwork. I think when you make an artwork and you put it out there, there's this uncertainty of 'this is part of me, I spent time on this.'"

Art Asks Us to Reflect on Complicated, Nuanced, and Ambiguous Ideas

Few other platforms and experiences can allow learners the reflective space to think about and create work that captures who they are in the world. A former student and novice educator, Leena echoed this sentiment: "The arts aren't always clear cut and there's not so much a right and wrong as there is room for interpretation and discussion . . . I think this is one of the reasons the arts are useful when it comes to learning about identity, community, and culture because they're topics that can be a little confusing and not quite clear cut and straightforward. Also the arts allow you to reflect back on ideas."

Art Is an Entry Point

There are works of art that connect with every single academic subject, human experience, cultural group, emotion, and perspective. We can use works of art to open the door to teach about any topic. No matter the subject, an artist somewhere at some point in time has addressed it. As Max, one of my former students, a muralist, and veteran teaching artist, declared, "[A]rt is a way . . . a kind of excuse. It's an 'in.' [I]t's a channel." When we turn our focus to identity, art gives everyone an entry point to begin (or continue) the conversation.

Art Humanizes Us

When I asked her why she uses art to teach about identity, Shannon replied, "The arts teach us about 'the life stuff.'" Given how art is so interwoven with what it means to be human, it can be a reminder of what makes us who we are. Musing about his own pedagogy, Mateo, another former student who is now a seasoned art teacher, suggested in our interview that we teach something more than just the skills of making things when we teach art:

> I feel as though I'm there for something more than just teaching you art. I'm here, and if today I have to share with you something important about being a human and it has nothing to do with art, then that's fine. I think our main purpose as art educators or educators in general is to make sure that students learn to be compassionate, caring human beings who value— who value people and who value life.

Writing about the responsibility of the artist, James Baldwin notes, "The precise role of the artist, then, is to illuminate that darkness, blaze roads through that vast forest, so that we will not, in all our doing, lose sight of its purpose, which is, after all, to make the world a more human dwelling place."[16] Through art, we often come to know each other as people and members of an interconnected community.

DESIGNING THE COURSE

In my first year at City College of New York in 2011, I was tasked with rewriting the curriculum for the graduate and undergraduate programs in art education. State requirements for certification provided clear guidelines for courses on human development, lesson planning, and literacy courses. However, as I thought about my own experiences in teaching and my research into youth perspectives on what makes effective educators, I realized something was missing. Certainly I could help students design lesson plans to meet specific learning goals, and there were opportunities for students to practice teaching and reflecting on their pedagogy. But how could I teach them that being an outstanding educator is so much more than lesson plans with seamless transitions and inventive strategies to assess student learning? How could I help them see that exceptional teaching requires us to value the relationships we have with our students and their communities in ways that we are rarely prepared for? How could I help them develop the tools to really get to know their students as the full, ever-changing, complex beings that we all are? How could I teach them the importance of building community? How could I prepare them to think critically about the social, cultural, economic, and political forces that shape each of us and our interactions with each other?

As I asked myself these questions, I realized that the answers were laid out in front of me. Sitting in the art education program office, surrounded by works of art—from both professional and novice artists—I remembered why I went into the arts. So often, through the production and engagement with art, people navigate the complexity, ambiguity, and messiness of what it means to be social creatures in the world together. Art both asks the question and tries to answer it: who are we (and will we be) to each other? Through poetry, imagery, movement, and performance, we learn and grapple with many of life's most complicated moments and relationships. Suddenly, I realized that the tools to teach educators how to develop critical and authentic relationships with students were embedded in the very content area I was supposed to be teaching. The challenge emerged: how could I explicitly use the practices and processes of making and looking at art to help students analyze who they were in relation to each other, their students, and society in order to foster real connections with their future students and the communities in which they would work?

To address these questions, I designed a course that would (hopefully) guide students through a series of activities and experiences to help them critique their own biases, while learning to connect with people who are somehow different. Like many justice-oriented educators today, I have poured over the scholarship of bell hooks, Bill Ayers, Paulo Freire, and Sonia Nieto in an effort to hone the theoretical and practical tools of critical social justice education and culturally responsive pedagogy. While reading about these important concepts has always been useful for me, I knew that the opportunity to experience building connections with real-life people would give students an even deeper understanding of how they could connect with their own future students and communities.

As I sat down to design a course that could equip arts educators with the awareness and skills to teach about and across difference, I was both sure of its necessity and nervous about how it would play out. With experiential learning in mind, I designed a semester-long "community engagement project" that I hoped would help arts educators analyze their own experiences as they practiced building a relationship with a community outside their typical social spheres. This community engagement project would provide a spine for the course by asking students to identify a community of people who they would try to get to know over the course of the semester.[17] I encouraged them to focus on communities outside their typical social circles and to seek the "edge of their comfort zone." To encourage them to foster intentional relationships with a chosen community, students in the course would complete a series of art activities ranging from looking closely at works of art, creating community maps, attending public events, visiting cultural organizations, researching local artists and community histories, reading fiction, and interviewing community members. Each activity would be interwoven with an artistic or written reflection through which students could analyze their experiences in light of theories on identity development, systemic oppression, and emancipatory education. In class, we would make art, closely observe contemporary artwork, and develop arts-based strategies for teaching about and across identity differences. Extensive readings on multicultural education, culturally relevant pedagogy, and liberatory educational theories would give students a theoretical foundation for our work. And throughout the entire experience, students would keep a journal using text and images to capture their evolving reflections in the course. I typed the syllabus and prepared for the first day.

FIRST SEMESTER

That spring, I somewhat anxiously greeted the first group of graduate students to enroll in "Identity, Community, and Culture in Art Education" at the City College of New York. The graduate students in the required course were a mix of current and preservice teachers. In many ways, they represented the cross-section of students in New York City schools, with the exception that almost all were women: several were Latina; there were some recent immigrants and some second- or third-generation transplants; a few identified as black or multiracial; a third or so identified as white; most were first-generation college and graduate students; many spoke more than one language; the majority identified as working, middle, or just-below-middle class; several were parents; all were eager to be the best teachers they could be to New York City's diverse population of students. Like almost every passionate educator I have met, these students were aware of the importance of their role as teachers and hungry to learn as many skills to help them succeed as champions of their students.

On the first day of class, I prepared the students for the semester ahead. As on any first day, the students were rather quiet as they took in the syllabus, my teaching style, and their classmates. We ran through some icebreakers and introductions. Together, we discussed a work of art for an hour. Finally, I introduced the premise of the semester-long "community engagement project." Fumbling my description of the project, I warned them that this was no anthropological endeavor; we were not studying "other" communities from afar. Rather, we were going to practice building relationships with people outside our regular circles, just as they would need to do as teachers. Suddenly the mood shifted. As we moved from theoretical conversations about how art can help us think about identity, difference, power, and community to the prospect of actually meeting and interacting with people different from them, the reality of the assignment sunk in: they were going to have to talk to strangers and it would likely be uncomfortable.

Despite their initial nervousness, students quickly warmed to the task. By the second session, they had written short essays about why they had selected the communities of people they hoped to get to know. Many of their responses were deeply personal:

- "My grandfather was a Holocaust survivor but I don't identify as Jewish, so I'm going to try to get to know people of the Jewish faith."
- "I teach in a school where almost all of my students are Dominican and I don't actually know much about their lives."
- "My best friend is transitioning from a female to male identity, and I'd like to be supportive, so I'm going to try to connect with people who identify as transgender."
- "I've lived in Bed-Stuy for six years and still don't know my neighbors."
- "My mother is Puerto Rican but she wouldn't let me speak Spanish at home. I'd like to know more about the local Puerto Rican community."
- "My father is in a nursing home and I have no idea what his life—or other seniors lives—are like!"

Others aimed at filling in blind spots related to their professional lives:

- "I've never really thought about what it means to teach art to people with vision impairments, so I'd like to gain a deep awareness of what it means to be blind."
- "I'm curious about the formal market-based art world since I never interact with people outside of art education."
- "I've always wondered why people choose to homeschool their children, so I'm going to try to hear their perspectives."
- "I think I often stereotype people who are devoutly religious, so I'd like to try to understand their faith more since I am sure I will have students who are religious."

As we discussed in class, a core function of their role as teachers is to be able to get to know their students and the families and communities of their students. Why not take the time to think about *how* to do this in ways that are affirming, honest, and critically compassionate? In naming the people they wanted to learn more about, the students grew excited. In reflection responses and class discussions, we talked about what their choices and trepidations told them about themselves. I asked them to consider why they had never reached out to these communities of people before. We talked about the nature of difference as a way of socially classifying and separating people and the many ways in which those lines are codified in our media, cultural practices, laws, economics, housing, and politics. Throughout the first three weeks, we had long discussions about works of art, such as Bernard Williams's *Charting America* and Carmen Lomas Garza's *Quinceñera*, to analyze artists' grappling with how we are taught about identity and difference in our culture. We created personal prints, blind contour drawings, and small collages, as we tried to unearth our own assumptions about the people the students would get to know—and about ourselves. Soon, the students were all immersed in getting to know people outside their typical social circles.

Halfway through that first semester of the course, I sat on the subway reading students' reflection papers and feeling a sense of relief. In getting to know people different from themselves, the students described small and seismic shifts in how they saw their roles as educators, artists, and citizens. While there was much in the course to tweak and revise, we were getting somewhere. At the midpoint of the fifteen-week semester, I made three columns on the board labeled "ah ha!" "surprised" and "puzzled." Neon-colored Post-it notes filled the space below each statement. I read them off one by one as we reflected on the progress of the course: "It wasn't as hard as I thought it would be." "I felt awkward at first, but then people were so warm and friendly to me." "My hands were sweaty and I wanted to turn around to leave, but then someone came over and welcomed me: 'We're glad you've joined us.'" Around the room, almost every comment was some variation on a theme: I did not want to intrude, reach out, or otherwise leave my comfort zone, but when I did, it was actually transformative for me (and maybe for the people I met). "Why is this?" I pondered aloud. Again, the comments echoed each other: "It's hard to break out of our social circles to meet people outside." "I didn't think we'd have anything in common." "We're taught to fear each other." "I never even thought to do it." In a country becoming increasingly segregated in our neighborhoods, media, schools, politics, and social interactions, the lines—both real and imaginary—that separate us prevent us from not only knowing each other, but also fully knowing ourselves.

At the end of the semester, as students reflected on their experiences with the community engagement project, their reactions were at turns emotional and analytical. Some participants talked about how their experiences prepared them to critically consider the importance of self-awareness and of creating caring, yet challenging spaces for talking about race, gender, and other identity factors. For example, a white museum educator reflected on the moments when she decides to bring up racial inequality and when she avoids it. Through discussing works of art, she realized that her decision is shaped by her own racial identity, which has caused her to talk explicitly about racial justice with her audiences. Other participants shared strategies for connecting with families via the arts and the simple importance of listening to what students create. Another former student, an African American teacher in Harlem, said she had realized that her portraiture assignments were threatening her Muslim students, whose religious beliefs forbade representations of the human form. She described her revised assignment and how she now researches the artwork from each student's cultural heritage in order to design more culturally relevant curricula. Still other participants described how creating art about identity raised their awareness of the structural inequalities linked to how we are labeled in our society. In thinking about when and why students are labeled as "students with learning disabilities," Paul, a white teacher and parent himself, described his own realization that the labeling of students is often tied to racial and economic power—or the lack thereof.

Nearly every student described some kind of growth. Several realized that their assumptions about the people they were getting to know were wildly off base. Many felt relieved that they had survived talking to strangers and reported a new sense of confidence in initiating conversations. Most described newly gained skills and strategies to connect with their future students, families, and communities. And everyone articulated clear connections to their teaching: they were more aware of their own biases, began to critically analyze structures of oppression that affect groups of people differently, knew how to break the ice with strangers, and recognized the importance of getting to know people in all of their complexity.

CRITIQUING THE COURSE

Since that first semester in 2011, I have taught the course ten times to almost 180 graduate and undergraduate students. While I alter the course each time, the core community engagement project has remained largely the same. Over fifteen weeks, students identify a community of people they would like to get to know better—preferably one they have had little previous connection to. I guide them through a series of scaffolded activities that help them connect with their community: they must go to a public event, talk with an insider, create a community map, read fiction, identify artists who emerge from the community, make a historical timeline, visit a public space of importance to the community, and finally, create a collaborative work of art. They follow each task with a written or artistic reflection on their experience. Meanwhile, the students read extensively about how difference, power, and privilege play out in education and in the arts and participate in facilitated conversations in which they unpack their experiences.

This experience is by no means perfect or flawless. It is actually, in many ways, a fraught exercise to intentionally foster connections across different social and cultural differences. As I describe when I discuss the challenges in the next chapter, there is great risk for harm when asking students to seek out people based on an assumed community or identity affiliation in an effort to learn more. We cannot ignore the history of othering people. And in this way, this entire project is inherently troubled. However, as educators, we are called to reach across various cultural and identity differences to teach. Even if we were to find ourselves in classrooms where students share our race, class, religion, gender, sexual orientation, and so forth, we would still likely be older or at least more academically trained than our students. Navigating difference of some sort will always be a part of our work as educators who seek to support our students' intellectual and social development. As many scholars have pointed out, we cannot *not* talk about it. Neutrality in education does not exist. So, we wade into what one student called the "uncharted waters" of trying to teach in ways that honor the unique social and cultural identities of our students (and ourselves). We cannot do this well if we don't take the time to consciously practice and hone our skills in teaching about and across difference.

MY BLIND SPOTS

Facilitating this course has taught me much about the ways in which we awkwardly bump into each other as we learn to understand, analyze, and connect with our many identities. I regularly make mistakes in teaching this course (more on those throughout the book). If I'm lucky, I recognize them myself or have a student or colleague point them out so I can try to readjust. But certainly many mistakes are caught in my own blind spots. I am a straight, able-bodied (for now), white, Christian-raised, cis-woman from an academically rich background, born in Michigan to rising middle-class American citizens, and living in New York City; my blind spots are admittedly large. Like many people from dominant identity groups who work toward racial, gender, and social justice, I struggle to unravel the privileges and powers given to me by a society built on oppressing people based on their race, class, gender, sexual orientation, religion, citizenship, class, ability, and whatever other categories it can find. To engage students in conversations about power and privilege, I too must be willing to be vulnerable, honest, and ever critical of the work we are trying to do. The courses I teach often involve high emotions. Sometimes people cry or leave the room, occasionally with hurt feelings. I try to be supportive while also holding us all—myself included—accountable to each other and to the communities with which we work. But however hard I try to be flexible, nimble, responsive, compassionate, patient, self-critical, analytical, and loving, I am, like my students, a product of the social systems that dominate our society. As I've tried to do in class, in writing this book I will do my best to point out my mistakes and those I try to avoid. I invite readers to shed light on any of the blind spots I've neglected.

Despite the messiness of trying to help educators gain the confidence and skills to navigate identity with their students and communities, the experience is well worth the risks. Like many education scholars, I believe it is our responsibility as educators to help each other navigate the uncharted and often turbulent waters of learning how to connect with each other across difference—with all the riptides and swells that come with the endeavor. In designing and teaching this course, I have witnessed profound changes in how students—preservice and veteran teachers—see themselves, their work, and their students. Alumni of the course consistently describe the ways in which they grew as people and educators as they learned to connect with people different from them. Ironically, by the end of the course, they often began to see those differences as socially constructed. By establishing real relationships with people from the communities they sought to know better, the fears about "others" dissipated; they often expressed a new excitement to find ways to learn more about their students' lives. According to their final reflections and the continued conversations I have with alumni of the course, students leave with the confidence and skills to nurture relationships with people across difference.

RESEARCHING THE BENEFITS

After that first semester of teaching "Identity, Community, and Culture in Art Education," I began to tell more people about my experience in the class. I was consistently curious about how students would describe their changing perceptions of themselves, their students, communities, and even professional responsibilities as educators and artists. The more I shared, the more

I wanted to know. Interested colleagues approached me for insight in using the arts to facilitate conversations about identity and community in their classrooms. Arts organizations began to inquire about professional development opportunities to build community among their staff and audiences. I realized I needed a better understanding of how the arts were helping my students develop the skills and sensibilities to connect with people across different social and cultural identities.

In 2015, I initiated a small qualitative research study to examine how current and preservice educators use the arts to deepen their understandings of themselves, their students, and their approach to teaching about and across identity. Working with alumni of the course, I conducted a series of in-depth, open-ended interviews about educators' reflections on using the arts to learn and teach about identity. In addition to the interviews, I analyzed student-generated writing and artwork as well as my own reflective notes from class discussions. The interviews with thirty-two alumni included a representative selection of students who typically take the course—from veteran educators to preservice teachers—and included some from every iteration of the course. Many participants were currently teaching art in schools, museums, and community centers in New York City.

Findings from this small study pointed to several emerging ideas for how the arts support learning about identity for both educators and their students.[18] Perhaps most importantly, in this arts-based course, nearly all participants described how their awareness of their own identity and the ways in which they could teach others about identity expanded and changed:

- "Professionally, my awareness of social and racial injustices, and my complicity in them, has been heightened. This has fostered important conversations with colleagues, and has made me more conscious of how I think about and speak to the audiences with whom I work."
- "This course opened my eyes to many of my own blind spots. I always considered myself someone socially, culturally aware, but . . . I am now always asking myself what am I missing because of my own positionality and how can I move beyond stereotypes and quick judgment to the individual."
- "I think that after taking this course . . . I have grown into a person who is able to stand my ground and react to racial comments either directed towards myself or others. I was less likely to do this in the past."

As course alumni described in greater detail how these changes unfolded, I began to see some key contributions that the arts offer to the endeavor of teaching about and across different social and cultural identities. Comparing these themes with existing scholarship, as I do in the following chapters, paints a compelling argument for the use of art—both making it and observing it—as a useful tool for teaching about identity and helping people learn to build critical and culturally responsive communities.

INTRODUCING STANCES

I played basketball and soccer as a child. In both sports, I spent countless hours practicing the right *stance* to be ready for the ball. My coaches trained me to lean in, keep my peripheral vision on both the ball and my teammates, and maintain near-constant motion. In sports, coaching about physical stance is a part of nurturing skilled athletes.

When I started listening to educators speak about their experiences learning to connect with people, I was taken back to my basketball and soccer years. As students talked about honing the skills they needed to teach about identity, they described actions such as "really listening" and "looking closely" that sound remarkably basic. Yet, they came to realize that there are specific ways of listening and looking that supported better relationships with their students. Just as my coaches showed me how to alter my center of gravity to help me become a more nimble athlete, the educators I spoke to saw the usefulness of seemingly subtle shifts in how they approached thinking, understanding, and teaching about identity. In adjusting their stances toward the work of getting to know themselves and their students, they were able to build stronger relationships. They described greater confidence in their ability to build supportive communities within their classrooms. Just as learning to correct my defensive stance and be a stronger ballplayer, educators can practice particular stances to become more effective educators.

This book introduces several stances for educators to practice on their own and with their colleagues, students, and members of the wider community. I chose the idea of stances for many reasons. First, I hope to highlight action; these are not simply mind-sets to bring to the work of teaching and learning about identity. My coaches didn't yell at me to just "be a good defender" or "score more"; they gave me specific activities to practice—even seemingly simple ones. To master a stance requires thoughtfulness. Second, to practice a stance is to develop a way of being. When we ask someone,

"What's your stance on this topic?" we're asking for their particular perspective. When we tend to our stances, we focus in on our unique position in the world—whether that's our physical stance in a soccer game or our emotional stance within a debate. Finally, I look to stances as a reminder of the need to practice and reflect on how we interact with each other. I think of being poised for action—ready to engage with the world.

Turning Inward and Leaning Outward

As I describe the stances we must cultivate to effectively teach and learn about identity, I draw from conversations with educators and my own experiences in teaching to highlight several art strategies for practicing these stances. I offer two kinds of strategies within each section. The first kind helps us turn a reflective eye on our own identities, assumptions, and biases. In *turning inward*, I encourage educators to become more critically aware of how their own identities shape their view of the world. Reflecting on this key move, Avery, a former student of mine, offered her thoughts: "My advice is for educators to start with themselves before asking students to consider identity, community and culture. Educators need to know where they stand within societal constructs and how that may affect their students, especially when bringing up topics of race, gender, oppression, and inclusion." Likewise, veteran educator Mateo encourages educators to begin with this work: "I would say first, deeply, richly, and profoundly explore your own identity, your core values, your belief system . . . I think if people truly know who they are and share from a loving point of view, that is going to be more contagious." Nearly every student I spoke with stressed the necessity of continually reflecting on our own selves if we are to effectively connect with and teach our students about and across our different identities. As writer Sonia Sanchez reminds us, "[Y]ou can't have relationships with other people until you give birth to yourself."[19]

Educators and scholars who work in fields such as multicultural education, critical race and queer theory, culturally responsive education, and social justice education advocate for critical self-reflection as a core component of effective teaching. They argue that educators must confront their own assumptions about their students if they hope to teach effectively. As Christopher Emdin writes, "Without teachers recognizing the biases they hold and how these biases impact the ways they see and teach students, there is no starting point to changing the dismal statistics related to the academic underperformance of urban youth."[20] Without this self-awareness, we risk reinforcing the very walls we aim to dismantle when we try to get to know each other. Extending the architectural metaphor, this double-edged work asks us to build connective bridges, while simultaneously deconstructing the borders those bridges span. If this task sounds figuratively challenging, it's because it is.

Once we have begun the work of turning inward to analyze our own perspectives on identity, then we can shift into *leaning outward*, the second kind of strategy, to better understand how we relate to those around us. In the second set of activities I include within each stance, I provide art-based strategies to help educators and students consider the relationships and connections they have with people, particularly those outside their typical social spheres. Through interacting directly with the world outside—the people, environments, and narratives—they come to see themselves and their interactions in a new light. I encourage educators, in leaning outward, to pay attention to how they move in the world, what they notice, who they encounter, and why. The combination of these two kinds of activities—turning inward and leaning outward—helps us nurture effective stances for teaching and learning about identity. Working together, the inward- and outward-facing stances provide a more complex awareness of how we relate with our students and how we can build culturally responsive communities that honor all of our identities.

℞ ℞ ℞

Quoting activist Grace Lee Boggs, writer Jeff Chang describes how Boggs envisioned the next revolution and what this asks of us: "As Grace Lee Boggs has put it, the next revolution might be better thought of as 'advancing humankind to a new stage of consciousness, creativity, and social and political responsibility.' Her revolution would require us to move away from finding new ways to divide and rule, and instead move toward honoring and transforming ourselves and our relations to each other."[21] While it may sound presumptuous to call getting to know each other better a revolutionary act, in a world where the socially constructed barriers between us seem to multiply and intensify each day, perhaps it is the best place to start if we have any hope of transforming barriers into bridges between us.

CHAPTER 1

Terms of Engagement

To bridge means loosening our borders, not closing off to others. Bridging is the work of opening the gate to the stranger, within and without. To step across the threshold is to be stripped of the illusion of safety because it moves us into unfamiliar territory and does not grant safe passage. To bridge is to attempt community, and for that we must risk being open to personal, political, and spiritual intimacy, to risk being wounded.[1]

—Gloria Anzaldúa

WHAT'S IN YOUR BACKPACK?

Everyone in class shuffles into the room with one or both shoulders weighed down by a bag or backpack. It's a sort of uniform for students. So, when I turn to the class one day to ask them to rustle through these bags and pull out an object that communicates something about themselves that the rest of us might not know, everyone starts rummaging. The objects vary: a tiny toy dinosaur, a grandmother's flowered handkerchief, a bold shade of lipstick, sunglasses, a clementine, a California-shaped keychain, a well-worn bracelet, a pencil case, a sketchbook, knotted headphones, a spork, and a smashed bumblebee in a Ziploc plastic bag. I ask the students to closely observe their object and make a contour drawing of what they see—basically just an outline of the object. Building directly on top of this outline, we use string, paper, and wire to create a raised drawing of the image and glue it onto a small square piece of cardboard. By adding materials to the page, we've created a textured surface to use to make a simple print. Students roll ink onto the raised surface and stamp it onto a blank page. As they remove the cardboard, they are left with a print of their string and wire drawing.

As the prints dry, I hand each student a stack of Post-it notes and ask them to take a moment to look silently at their peers' prints. For each image, I instruct them to leave a note that describes what they think the owner of the object and the maker of the image care about or what kind of person they might be. I turn on some music as they get out of their seats. Students lean into the prints with their heads turned slightly sideways, or step back to examine each image. On the Post-its, they write their immediate guesses: "relishes routine" near the spork; "has hometown pride" near the California keychain; "introverted" by the headphones; "creative" by the sketchbook; and "science lover" by the crushed bumblebee. As the Post-its stack up next to each image, the responses vary. The owner of the headphones is also seen as a "messy music lover" and "careless with objects." The owner of the toy dinosaur is seen as a "parent," a "kid at heart," and a "hoarder." By the time the students have noted their initial reactions to each image, the pile of Post-it notes begins to point to the multiple ways in which each image conveys meaning to the people in the room.

We end the activity with each student sharing the response that fits him or her most closely and the one that is most off the mark. As they share, several students remark that they hadn't ever thought that the object they hold dearly could also be seen as conveying another meaning: "I treated myself to this bold new lipstick as a reward for a good grade I received, so I was surprised that someone thought I might be a 'party girl.'" Others point out that, in seeing their object through the eyes of a classmate, they had come to view themselves in a different light: "I hadn't ever thought that I value routines, but now that you mention it, I do eat my lunch with this same spork every day." As we complete the activity, we discuss how our first impressions are always shaped by our biases and assumptions—many of them formed by media and previous experiences that limit our views of people. Making art about these impressions enables us to bring these biases into the open to be able to see and analyze them. In reflecting on this activity, Max recalled how an art-making activity that "was very abstract" and rather "subjective, ultimately showed how little you can base assumptions about people based on who you think they are."

TERMS OF ENGAGEMENT

As one of the first activities I facilitate with students, the prints of the backpack objects offer us an opening to talk about the terms of engagement for using art to navigate our own and each other's identities. Talking about identity and difference is challenging in even the best of circumstances. We are conditioned to both secretly obsess about and publicly try to ignore discussions of identity. Because of this, many of us enter the classroom (both as students and educators) with only a surface awareness of our own identities, unaware of how both internal and external forces shape those identities. Activist and writer Audre Lorde writes:

> [W]e have all been programmed to respond to the human differences between us with fear and loathing and to handle that difference in one of three ways: ignore it, and if that is not possible, copy it if we think it is dominant, or destroy it if we think it is subordinate. But we have no patterns for relating across our human differences as equals. As a result, those differences have been misnamed and misused in the service of separation and confusion. Certainly there are very real differences between us of race, age, and sex. But it is not those differences between us that are separating us. It is rather our refusal to recognize those differences, and to examine the distortions which result from our misnaming them and their effects upon human behavior and expectation.[2]

Whether it is driven by fear, awkwardness, shame, pride, or ignorance, the reticence to even talk about identity is a very real obstacle to teaching and learning about who we are and how we can coexist with people different from us. Lorde reminds us that "too often, we pour the energy needed for recognizing and exploring difference into pretending those differences are insurmountable barriers, or that they do not exist at all. This results in a voluntary isolation, or false and treacherous connections. Either way, we do not develop tools for using human difference as a springboard for creative change within our lives."[3] Acknowledging how challenging this work can be and the need to develop such tools for creative change is a good place for us to start.

To prepare for this work, we establish some ground rules or expectations. In naming the terms of engagement, I aim to remind students of the attitudes and understandings we must bring to teaching and learning about identity in our efforts to build thriving diverse communities. My interviews with students underscored these foundational principles. Many spoke of how they had never considered the need to bring such intentionality to their attempts to get to know their students and to nurture healthy communities of learners. While I introduce the concepts that follow on the first day of the course experience, we cycle back to them throughout the entire semester. In many ways, they serve as parameters for the work of learning and teaching about identity—reminders of the mind-sets we must nurture as we go. Here I outline how we introduce them through the lens of making and talking about art.

Recognize That Identity Is Constantly Changing

When students search through their backpacks to identify an object, I watch as they pull out a variety of things, sometimes holding one for a second to ponder it before passing it over for something else dug up from the bottom. Having done this activity myself, I can almost hear some of their thoughts: "Does this represent me?" "Wait, what is this doing in here?" "What do I want to share about myself?" "Oh, this one is too embarrassing." "No one will understand this." Thoughts such as these highlight the ever-shifting nature of identity. The artifacts we carry with us may be appropriate in one setting, carry historical or sentimental meaning in another, or project a particular story in yet another. We discuss in class what educators Gwyn Kirk and Margo Ŏkazawa-Rey have written: "Identity formation is the result of a complex interplay among a range of factors: individual decisions and choices, particular life events, community recognition and expectations, societal categorization, classification and socialization, and key national or international events"; identity is an ever-evolving mix of who we think we are and who others think we are.[4]

Kirk and Ŏkazawa-Rey describe three layers of identity to highlight the many factors at play in determining who each of us is in the world. The micro-level relates to our own views of who we are—our personalities, life experiences, and claimed identifiers. We might be siblings and introverts. We could be survivors of trauma and champion chess players. We may describe ourselves as black and feminist. Often, as students rummage through their backpacks for objects to share, they are thinking first of these personal micro-identities. Maybe they are proud of being a parent, so they pull out that toy dinosaur to share. Or perhaps they want to convey their hidden musical talents, so they pull out a guitar pick. In doing so, they are making public the so-called micro-identities that they hold dear.

As they share the printed images of their identity objects, we encounter what Kirk and Ŏkazawa-Rey term the "meso" or community level of identity. Here our various personal identities interact and intersect with those around us. Kirk and Ōkazawa-Rey write, "At the community level, individual identities and needs meet group standards, expectations, obligations, responsibilities, and demands."[5] In other words, they remind us, "You compare yourself with others and are subtly compared."[6] When students create images of their original objects, they are typically proud of the identities they intend to share. Once we share their images—prints that end up being visual distortions of the original objects—we encounter the group comparisons of the meso-level of identity. Using the images, we can talk about our associations with particular groups of people. Artists who are expected to always carry sketchbooks, people we assume to be religious because of the crosses on their key chains. As we discuss these assumptions, we learn more about each other. Sometimes our assumptions end up being good guesses, and other times we are way off. Yes, that well-worn sketchbook belongs to an artist, but the cross key chain was a gift from a beloved friend. Through these conversations, we see how we are constantly engaged in a process of trying to sort out who we are in relation to the people around us, based on the social cues we both project and receive.

As we talk about the assumptions we made about people based on their artworks, inevitably someone will mention a larger social grouping such as race, class, gender, sexual orientation, or ability. These macro-level identity categories are the dominant socially constructed labels we each learn from the moment we are born. Typically based on real or imagined aspects of our natural physical, genetic, or biological identities, these socially imposed classifications are designed to determine who belongs to one group and not to another. They are meant to prescribe specific roles, status, power, responsibility, and privilege to preestablished groups of people (usually over other groups of people). As Kirk and Ōkazawa-Rey describe, these social categories are "used to establish and maintain a particular kind of social order."[7] Encoded in our history, cultural codes, and systems of power, they remind us that the identity categories of the macro-level have been employed "to justify the conquest, colonization, domination, and exploitation of entire groups of people, and although the specifics may have changed over time, this system of categorizing and classifying remains intact."[8] Precisely because of this history of oppression, educators must pay special attention to the ways in which these macro-level identities affect our relationships with students. In our conversation about the associations we have about each of these categories, students can begin to more critically analyze their significance in their own lives and the lives of their own students and communities.

In talking about our terms of engagement, the backpack-object activity highlights the many ways in which our identities are constantly shifting, contextual, intersectional, and multilayered. With this understanding, we can practice meeting our students, their families, and our communities in the moment to understand who they are right now. We can learn to recognize and analyze the labels that we are taught to bestow on each other and the social expectations, associations, and roles linked to those labels. We can see those labels for what they are—categories to group and divide us. In doing so, we can move closer to a more complex understanding of how our various identities play out in our own lives and in the lives of those around us.

Move from Seeing People as Other to Another

In her essay "Eating the Other," bell hooks describes the danger of identifying people by the socially constructed categories that have been used to exploit and oppress people in order to interact with, encounter, or engage with them. Citing examples from film, television, advertising, and everyday interactions, she highlights how often people within positions of power seek out those who are racially or culturally different from those in power in order to consume, experience, or learn from their difference: "The commodification of Otherness has been so successful because it is offered as a new delight, more intense, more satisfying than normal ways of doing and feeling. Within commodity culture, ethnicity becomes spice, seasoning that can liven up the dull dish that is mainstream white culture."[9] Put simply, we must beware the urge to treat people as exotically *other* than us.

Clearly, this tendency to turn other people into objects to be consumed not only is highly problematic, but also prevents any kind of reciprocal relationship building. As educators seek to nurture honest, caring, and supportive relationships with students across their many identities, they must develop a critical lens for how they conceptualize people who are somehow different than they are. Part of this requires acknowledging the moments when we do think of people as other. As Leena, a former student, reflected: "Before I might push away thoughts that come up about other people, but now I let myself admit conceptions I have about a person, and then will examine why these initial thoughts might have come up." Moving beyond this necessitates a shift from thinking about people as *other* to thinking about them as *another*—another person to learn from, grow with, and care for.

When students respond to the prompt "What does this image tell you about the maker?" they often jot down their immediate assumptions in the form of categorizations of people: "they are messy," "they are hoarders," or "they are from California." The objectification of people into categories comes quickly to us. We can easily turn our classmates into others who are simply defined by the labels we give them. Yet, when we start to discuss these responses aloud and in front of our peers, the nuances start to emerge. What appeared as messiness to one student was actually creativity to another. The hoarder may also be viewed as a collector and the Californian as someone with hometown pride. As students talk about their initial assumptions about each other based on their artworks, they realize that what one might have seen as otherness, as some categorical difference, might actually be closer to a characteristic they also share. They see the multiple interpretations of identity. They see connections between and across their works of art—and in doing so, across their own identities. The other becomes another.

This is not to say that our unique experiences as social creatures have no meaning—quite the contrary. Our identities do have meaning, but those meanings are not as concrete as we are often taught. Furthermore, the labels that we attribute to each other are not portals into other worlds. As educators—as people—we must be wary of the weight we give to the labels we ascribe to each other since they are too often used to turn people into others. As hooks warns, "[T]he over-riding fear is that cultural, ethnic, and racial differences will be continually commodified and offered up as new dishes to enhance the white palate—that the Other will be eaten, consumed, and forgotten."[10] Certainly, our particular identities have significance; however, they are not our only feature; nor should we treat each other as if they are.

For educators then, the question becomes, how do we learn to connect with people who we are trained to view as categorically different from us? Part of it is understanding that we do use the lenses of difference and otherness, despite our best intentions. From there, we can challenge ourselves to create connections with people that allow for both an awareness of our differences and a belief that we can find points of convergence. This requires an intentional commitment to valuing some not just as an *other*, but as *another*. Discussing this shift, Olivia, a former student from my course, who speaks only English, reflected on her attempts to connect with the Spanish-speaking community within her own church: "I want to reflect my respect for them—like in valuing their responses, their expressions, with the whole

. . . sharing with them, making sure the whole group is hearing that. So the whole group can see that I'm valuing them." Here, the challenge is that in Olivia's hope of connection with a group of people that at one point felt other to her, she is asking them, as hooks writes, "to be both witness and participant in [her] transformation."[11]

What, then, is the well-meaning and critically thinking educator to do to ensure that she is not exploiting the otherness of her students in order to learn and teach about identity? In class, we talk about strategies to find points of entry for conversation with new people. Using our experiences talking about each other's artworks, I encourage my students to find common areas of interest upon which they might build a relationship with someone, rather than try to consume them. Describing the challenge of trying to get to know people outside her typical social circles, Jasmin, a high school teacher and student in the class, ponders how she initiates a conversation across difference:

> How to talk to people? Okay, so first like, it's gonna be this weird phase 'Cause you can't just walk up to people like, "Hey, I need to know white people" and they're going to be like, "She's crazy, get outta here!" [Start to observe] this person until you notice something that has nothing to do with the thing [their otherness] and then that's the entry point. Like, "Oh my gosh! She eats hot dogs, so do I." "Do you want to go to Nathan's [hot dog restaurant] with me? And possibly talk about race and gender and socioeconomic status over like dogs and chili?" So, it's about finding an entry point . . . Like, I know that I used to be scared to talk to someone who identifies as homosexual, so I cannot approach them immediately with all these questions about homosexuality written down in a list. I have to find another common place so that they can trust me enough to want to answer those questions and I could trust myself enough to say something that's not offensive.

In addition to seeking points of connection, educators must also bring a critical awareness of the power dynamics at play when teaching and learning about identity. Writing about the unequal power between racial categories in the United States, hooks reminds us "[t]hat simply by expressing their desire for 'intimate' contact with black people, white people do not eradicate the politics of racial domination as they are made manifest in personal interaction."[12] In other words, the good intentions of trying to get to know people outside our social circles simply because they *are* outside those circles will not prevent us from doing harm. hooks continues with a suggestion for how to avoid othering: "Mutual recognition of racism, its impact both on those who are dominated and those who dominate, is the only standpoint that makes possible an encounter between races that is not based on denial and fantasy."[13] Here, she points to a key term of engagement for teaching and learning about and across different identities: we must constantly tend to the power dynamics associated with our various identities as we seek to meet each other for who we are. Just as the educator-students in my class practiced talking about how their own identities shaped the multiple layers and possible interpretations of their object prints, they must bring a similar level of analysis to their interactions with their students and the extended communities with whom they work.

All discussions of identity require critical engagement with concepts of power and privilege. Because of how our many identities have so often been used to classify, divide, and privilege some groups of people over others, we cannot understand who we each are without also talking about how, when, and why we have power based on our identity (and when we don't). This task requires historical, economic, political, and cultural analyses of the power dynamics assigned to different identities. When we neglect these multifaceted analyses, our discussions of identity remain simplistic and potentially harmful. To build bridges to connect people of different identity groups, we must understand how asymmetrical power relationships shape who we are in relation to each other. Only then can we begin to form more nuanced and layered understandings of how identity informs our lives.

Seek Discomfort, Vulnerability, and Trust

There's almost always a momentary silence when I ask students to create an image based on the objects they have pulled from their backpacks. Since many of them are artists and educators already, they know that when I ask them to create something, I will assuredly ask them to share it publicly. Whatever they make will be seen. As anyone who has ever created anything—be it a drawing, a poem, a song, or a dance—letting other people see it can be incredibly daunting. It often takes a fair amount of courage and a capacity to make oneself vulnerable, since we can never really know what others will think of our work. Understanding this leap of faith into discomfort and the trust it necessitates is another important term of engagement when using art to teach and learn about identity.

To create art requires a particular kind of faith in oneself and one's audience—whether that audience is a friend, classmate, teacher, colleague, or the greater public. As Jasmin points out, "Art is supposed to be like one of the most intimate parts of a person, right? You're using whatever knowledge that you know about any particular range or combination of subjects to make a piece of something that's like, completely yours. That's an extension of your identity. So, in order to share something like that with somebody, you have to have your guard down, a little. That's where the trust comes in." In each class and workshop and nearly every interview, students I have worked with describe how the process of making art is one of intense vulnerability. This vulnerability requires trust in oneself and one's viewers.

Thinking about her own artistic process, Stefanie, a former student, describes the sense of fear she often experiences when confronting a fresh page: "Something I struggled with a lot is getting started . . . you're sitting and you just look at that blank sheet of paper and making the first mark seems kind of terrifying." Her description of the fear of starting a work of art runs parallel to the ways in which many people fear talking about their identity or the identities of others. As Jane, another student from my course, reflected on the experience of confronting her own identity, she described the fear of "finding out, so who am I? . . . And who am I in relation to others?" Making art then becomes a space to practice that sense of vulnerability and to cultivate a sense of trust in talking about and thinking about who we are.

In our moments of discomfort, we often learn the most. The moments in life when we make mistakes—we hurt a friend's feelings, we miss curfew, we fail a class, we drop the ball—are usually those when we achingly grow in our understandings of ourselves and each other. As uncomfortable as these moments are, we often look back upon them knowing that, truly, what didn't kill us certainly made us stronger, more thoughtful, and more aware. The work of educators is often to help students brave these moments. We ask students to step into the discomfort of learning when we ask them, in front of their peers, to answer a question about a new topic, or to work with a classmate with whom they don't get along. We celebrate the moments of discomfort when we ask students to describe aloud what they see in an abstract poem or work of art or when we encourage them to get on stage and perform or dance in front of an audience. We do this not to be cruel, but because education theories tell us that we learn when we are forced out of our comfort zones. We want our students to succeed, so we encourage them to try, even if trying might mean failing.

When I finally call on students to share their identity object prints, I can often feel their reticence. They might preface their work with a statement about how it didn't turn out as they had planned, or that they could do better if they had more time. Anything to dilute their discomfort. However, this discomfort is right where we want to be. I often encourage students to lean into this discomfort—to trust its capacity to help us learn. Nowhere is this as important as when we teach and learn about identity and difference. In the United States, we are often taught—consciously and unconsciously—to avoid the discomfort of talking about who we are in relation to other people. But as I discussed in the introduction, the only way to change this fear about identity is to embrace the discomfort of talking about it. Writing about how to upend the imbalanced power dynamics in teaching, educator and scholar Lisa Delpit eloquently names this vulnerability as an imperative, yet one that requires tremendous work: "[W]e must learn to be vulnerable enough to allow our world to turn upside down in order to allow the realities of others to edge themselves into our consciousness."[14] Delpit reminds readers that this kind of vulnerability requires educators to step outside themselves to critically analyze their own identities—a challenge that can feel as if you've lost solid ground beneath your feet.

When students talk about the discomfort and vulnerability of making art, their comments parallel those I often hear when people talk about why they avoid teaching and learning about identity. Both activities inspire some amount of anxiety, and both require a healthy dose of trust. A certain baring of the heart comes with these two actions. Making and looking at art can function as a place for us to practice stepping into the space of vulnerability and discomfort we need to deepen our understanding of identity and how it manifests in our students' lives and our own. Discussing the need to "get comfortable with being uncomfortable," Jasmin describes how "you must have had to experience being uncomfortable before to know if you're ready to be that uncomfortable or more uncomfortable than that again." Art gives us a rehearsal space for the discomfort of engaging with the meaning of our identities.

In laying out our terms of engagement for teaching and learning about identity, the move to aim for discomfort always sounds a bit odd. Yet, as Jasmin states, it's "weird 'cause nobody wants to be uncomfortable. But it's basically where most learning happens: when you're most uncomfortable." Like making art, the good stuff happens when we trust ourselves (and each other) to lean into the vulnerability and discomfort of questioning who we all are.

Real education about identity—the kind that can be transformational—requires hard and sustained work. This is not the stuff of a single lesson plan or an afternoon professional development workshop. To teach and learn about identity, one must be prepared to be uncomfortable, patient, and persistent. Often, I remind my students of educators and diversity facilitators Brian Arao and Kristi Clemens's call to move from "safe spaces to brave spaces."[15] Safe conversations are often surface-level conversations about identity, never dipping below to reach the complex, nuanced, sometimes contradictory, power-laden, and emotional depths of our identities. Skimming the surface risks perpetuating stereotypes and false narratives, thereby further damaging our sense of who we are in relation to each other. Critical educator-scholar Leigh Patel reminds us that "[l]earning involves departing from known automatic practices, venturing into experiences that aren't wholly predictable, and experiencing temporary, productive failure."[16] To truly transform our understanding of our identities, we must bravely lean into the discomfort of being vulnerable with each other, risking failure by engaging with honesty and humility.

Embrace Messiness and Ambiguity

Something interesting happens when students first lift the collaged cardboard to reveal their printed image: they are usually either delighted or somewhat disappointed. "Huh, that was not what I expected," someone will exclaim. Nearly every artist, dancer, performer, writer, or creator has a story about how the reality of their artwork did not match their initial vision for their creation. Mistakes happen. Materials are missing or don't quite work as anticipated. Accidental sounds arise (and might be preferred). Something spills or is torn. Someone forgets a line and improvises. And then, oddly enough, the creation takes on a new shape; some unexpected artwork emerges. Such is the nature of creative production.

The ambiguity and unpredictability of making art underscores another key term of engagement. To teach and learn about identity requires an acceptance of the messiness of the process. As in art, when talking about identity, there are rarely easy or clear-cut answers. Multiple interpretations can be hotly debated. Seemingly contradictory truths can coexist. And mistakes happen just as often. Someone repeats a stereotype they had never critically analyzed. Someone else misunderstands a comment and retreats. The responses we imagine are rarely the ones we end up hearing. One idea falls flat but reveals another. Someone's view of the world is challenged, perhaps shattered. Then, oddly enough, the discussion takes on a new shape; some unexpected understanding emerges. Such is the nature of teaching and learning about identity.

As the students read the Post-its containing classmates' reactions to their object prints, all were immediately struck by the ambiguity of the images. "I guess I saw it differently," one student said. Another piped up: "I looked at this print and saw what I wanted to see." These comments point to the ways in which art can highlight the ambiguous and shifting nature of our identities. Students typically make this connection quickly. "It's just like how people always assume that I'm white, even though I'm actually Puerto Rican," said one student. Another chimes in, "Yes, I realized that I bring my own assumptions and lenses to see what I want to see in your artwork." In this way, students start to confront the ways in which our identities are not always what they seem on the surface. Along with this, they notice how alternative explanations and interpretations are possible. They see the messiness of identity.

As educators, we must remember that mistakes happen, messiness can be productive, ambiguity might actually be the answer, and unpredictability may lead us where we need to go. Just as artists learn to sit with the frustrations that arise from now knowing the end result from the beginning, so too must educators embrace the lack of a linear path. Reflecting on his attempts to get to know new people, Chris, a novice educator, describes: "It wasn't really mapped out what it would look like, so I had to improvise . . . it's not a clean trajectory, so it's messy. It's accidental. It kind of twists and turns and I really felt like I had to follow that. I had to be attentive to where my openings were." I do not underestimate the challenge of this. In classrooms where teachers must submit regular lesson plans, order supplies in advance, work within a calculated bell system, not to mention meet state and national standards via a regular testing structure, there is little room for missteps, wiggle room, or surprise. Furthermore, rarely are teachers encouraged to relinquish some control over their teaching. More commonly, they are told to gain tighter control over their students, pedagogy, and classroom management. Such tight reins do little to help us explore the messiness of understanding who we each are in relation to each other—let alone learn to build community within and across our various identities.

Messiness and ambiguity are therefore critical terms of engagement in any attempt to teach and learn about identity. Without space to figuratively bump into each other, we will not learn how to analyze why we often collide or how to move together without harm. As in art, without mistakes we would not experience the leaps of creative thinking and imagination that have resulted in some of the most profound works of poetry, visual art, and performance. At the risk of sounding dramatic, from within the mess, we often find our clarity.

COMMON CHALLENGES

Given the complexity of identity, any attempt to teach about who we are and to build relationships with people who are somehow different from us is bound to risk perpetuating the very kinds of oppressive behaviors we may be trying to dismantle. No matter how closely we adhere to the terms of engagement, challenges arise. As I've come to understand over several years of helping educators develop the skills to get to know their students and their communities, there are a few key areas of potential harm that I outline below. In describing these challenges, I do not mean to deter others; rather I offer them as reminders of areas to pay particular attention to as we intentionally get to know people outside our typical social circles. Luckily, because this book focuses on how the arts can help us think about who we are in relation to each other, the arts often provide opportunities to address these challenges in creative and productive ways.

Not Anthropology, Not Colonialism

A primary risk in setting up an intentional get-to-know-someone experience within the context of school is the prospect of the anthropological turn. An attempt to learn about a group of people has the potential of devolving quickly into an experiment in discovery science, whereby the students sees themselves as inquisitive outsiders taking notes on and observing specimens "in their natural habitat." This problematic approach creates a distance between the students and the people they hope to get to know. Further, it also maintains the power dynamics that might already exist within the relationship. Treating the task as one in which we are trying to get information about people, rather than actually build a reciprocal and mutually respectful relationship with someone, sets up a situation in which the student is simply taking from people. It is a slippery slope to replicating the kinds of colonial practices of people in power worldwide whereby outsiders enter a community and demand something of value (knowledge, property, land, information, skills, etc.) without offering or exchanging anything in return. To approach the task in this way would simply replicate the very oppressive social patterns that so often keep different groups of people from interacting in the first place. It risks damaging not only the student's potential for nuanced understanding of and connection with a group of people, but it could also exacerbate and reinforce the existing divisions between groups of people.

To attend to this potential pitfall, we spend significant time in class to prepare for the community engagement project by discussing the dangers of an anthropological stance and the challenges of entering a community as an outsider. Educators seeking to introduce a similar project might consult the scholarship of educator-scholars Linda Tahiri-Smith, Leigh Patel, and Eve Tuck. Here, the arts offer an excellent point of departure for conversations about the anthropological or colonial gaze. One might begin with a close analysis of Edward Curtis's problematic photographs of Native American people from the early 1900s, which were included in his widely celebrated and critiqued multivolume publication, *The North American Indian*.[17] This collection of photographs, sponsored by J. P. Morgan, sought to document what Curtis thought was a "vanishing race" of people. The images present a romanticized and colonial view of what it meant to be Native American at the turn of the century—all through the eyes of a white outsider. A close analysis of these photographs, especially compared to the contemporary work of photographers such as Wendy Red Star and Will Wilson, who both identify as Native American and respond to Curtis's images in their own photography, can provide an opportunity for learners to consider what it means to be viewed through someone else's lens.

As I introduce the community engagement project in my class, we discuss the nebulous definition of community and consider the many communities they identify with. We cover the whiteboard with various possible community identifiers: New Yorker, student, woman, Korean American, queer, first-generation immigrant, restaurant worker, Christian, veteran, Democrat, bilingual, environmentalist, black, only child, Muslim, artist, educator, recovering addict, and parent. As we compare these various identifiers, we talk about the differences between communities that emerge from shared interests, affinities, roles, or personal choices and those that we are born into based upon socially constructed categories. What, we debate, does it mean to name a community from the position of being outside that community?

Who are we to say that a particular group of people is a community? How are we extending the colonial mind-set by assuming that a group of people is a community? In these conversations, I urge students to reflect critically about the many ways in which they may unconsciously replicate anthropological or colonial ways of interacting with people and to consider ways to alter their behaviors.

To help students practice building relationships with people outside their social circles, I allow them to identify any community with whom they would like to connect. This is admittedly problematic. However, it also mimics the ways in which educators encounter students in their classrooms: often, as educators, we assume that our students belong to particular communities, and only upon engaging with them more closely do we learn about their more nuanced and complex relationships with these assumed communities. So, my students are left to identify groups of people they would like to get to know—from the community of dancers in New York City or the homeschool community to recently immigrated Coptic Christians or transgender youth. As they make their choices, I ask them to reflect critically about those choices and to interrogate their own assumptions as they get to know people better. We do not entirely avoid this pitfall, but as educators who will undoubtedly need to learn about the lives and cultures of our students, we must learn to be wary of the anthropological gaze. As artist Lucy Lippard reminds us when she writes about the unfolding and complex nature of working with communities of people, "Community doesn't mean understanding every-thing about everyone and resolving all the differences; it means knowing how to work within differences as they evolve and change."[18] Throughout this book, I offer my best attempts to mitigate the risks through encouraging constant reflection, humility, and honesty—the very same qualities we hope to embody as exceptional educators.

Edge of Your Comfort Zone

The prompt to get to know people at "the edge of your comfort zone" has proven to be one of the most important and the most tenuous elements of the community engagement project. As I explain in class, I encourage students to think about their typical social spheres and to consider who is left out of those spheres: who do they avoid, either consciously or not? As they identify their own opportunities for learning, I urge students to choose a community that has personal meaning for them, yet one with which they have had little opportunity to develop deep understanding. What results is that students often identify communities of people about whom they have many misconceptions and biases. This runs the risk of allowing them to act on those false assumptions once they encounter actual people. Again, we see how this could perpetuate some of the stereotypes and beliefs we are trying to break down as we meet people across socially constructed categories. However, this task also parallels exactly what teachers will encounter in their professional lives when they have the responsibility to educate diverse groups of students. Far too often, educators in classrooms across the United States act on the false narratives they have invented or have been taught about their students. These biases color every interaction they have with students and students' extended communities. As Delpit eloquently writes, "We do not really see through our eyes or hear through our ears, but through our beliefs."[19] Years of facilitating antibias and antiracism workshops have taught me that we must first identify our beliefs and biases in order to dismantle them.

The opportunity to get to know people outside their comfort zone requires students to name their comfort zone. As they do, they gain a greater understanding of their own limited awareness of people and become more consciously aware of the ways in which they are uncomfortable. When I ask students to intentionally embrace the discomfort in getting to know people outside their social circles, I create a space for them to acknowledge and use that discomfort for their own growth. Here, again, the arts can be a useful point of reference. Since making art often requires a certain amount of risk taking and discomfort, educators preparing to meet new people might use some simple art-making activities to practice leaning into discomfort. Blind contour portraits—images created by drawing an outline of a person or object without looking at the page—can help even nonartists practice the kind of vulnerability they need to meet relative strangers.

While nothing can entirely remove the element of artificiality in the assignment of building relationships across difference, we can aim for reciprocity, exchange, respect, and mutuality as we cross the socially constructed barriers between groups. For example, in class, we discuss strategies for approaching people that demonstrate respect and a genuine willingness to connect. While many students point to the assignment as the impetus for initiating a conversation, they include their personal reasons for building a relationship across difference. In articulating their personal and professional hopes for getting to know a community, they practice honesty, vulnerability, and openness in their initial encounters. In the best cases, students have found ways of reaching out to people different from them by finding points of mutual connection. One student joined an early-morning running club for people in transitional housing. Another student signed up for a ceramics class for people with vision impairments. These students found ways to meet people outside their comfort zones by starting with shared interests. Such seemingly small moves help lay a foundation that may help avert some of the harm associated with a more invasive entry into a new community.

Knowing Others to Know Ourselves

What I didn't say on that first day of class (but do now) was that this course, with its community engagement project, was designed to help students learn about themselves—to help them identify how difference, power, and privilege color their relationships with other people and with their own identities. The hazard here is that we run the risk of using others as props to learn about ourselves. The act of othering people, as I mentioned previously and will return to again in subsequent chapters, is highly problematic. In naming someone as "other," we highlight the divides between us. Such divisions are socially constructed and perpetuated. Nobel Peace Prize winner and anti-apartheid activist Desmond Tutu writes often about the concept of inter-connectivity: "*Ubuntu* is very difficult to render into a Western language. It speaks of the very essence of being human . . . It is to say, 'My humanity is caught up, is inextricably bound up, in yours.' We belong in a bundle of life. We say, 'A person is a person through other persons.' It says: 'I am human because I belong. I participate, I share.'[20] In direct opposition to this concept of *ubuntu*, when we other someone, we deny the ways in which our existences are tied to others: we all exist in relation to each other. While the concept of individuality is highly prized in many Western (namely white) communities, the notion that we can each exist as fully independent beings is improbable. Humans are social creatures whose existence depends on the connections—both acknowledged and denied or ignored—between us.

The premise of the community engagement project is that we are interdependent beings, belonging "in a bundle of life," as Desmond Tutu writes.[21] To know ourselves requires that we know each other. However, without an understanding of this concept, students might fall prey to the belief that they are separate from the people around them. This perspective can quickly slip into seeing other people as lesser or not warranting the kind of compassionate care that they afford those they consider as their "own kind." To counter this, we use the tools of critical reflection to constantly remind ourselves of the ways in which people are inherently interdependent. Because every culture produces some form of art (whether or not it is called that is a subject for another book), looking at and making art can remind us of the ways in which we often share more than we are taught. Examining how artists create work about common human themes such as birth, love, and death can spark conversations about shared life experiences. Additionally, close analyses of works such as artist Kara Walker's silhouettes or Firelei Báez's "Can I Pass? Introducing the Paper Bag to the Fan Test for the Month of December" can point to the ways in which even in our worst moments, humans are inextricably bound to each other. War, slavery, sexism, and even everyday stereotypes ensnare us all, with some of us in positions of power and others subject to that power.

Throughout my work with educators, I return often to these ideas as I encourage people to teach about and across different social and cultural identities. As we strive to build diverse communities of learners, we will inevitably need to interact with people who are different from us. We can think about them as separate entities—others in the negative sense—or as partners in our own existence. When we make this shift, we can be open to learning about ourselves in new ways and can build genuine relationships with those around us.

These challenges are tied to the very premise of a project designed to help people think about their own social and cultural identities and to learn how to teach about and build communities across those identities. As an educator, I regularly trip over them myself. I name them here to flag them for others. There is no perfect way of diving into the ways of teaching about identity. The course I teach is certainly a work in progress—one with many lessons to share from both the stories of growth and the pitfalls along the way. This book attempts to document these lessons in hopes that other educators will build on and adapt them in their own contexts.

❧ ❧ ❧

At the end of the first day, students tuck their prints into their folders and toss their objects back into their bags. It's easy to pocket these artifacts of our identities. However, by the next week, their impressions remain. Someone asks the toy dinosaur owner about her daughter. Someone else has brought in clementines to share with the class. I overhear a joke about bumblebees. A few students pull out their prints to reexamine them. One student wonders aloud that her image no longer looks like her pencil case; it has taken on new meaning and now looks entirely different. Our identities shift. Someone looks over and offers another interpretation. There is some debate, a little disagreement. Someone else laughs as she refers to the terms of engagement—the messiness and the vulnerability. And like that, we have opened the door for the next session.

CHAPTER 2

Noticing Stance

It has to do with being comfortable with the notion that the world is complicated and full of grays, but there's still truth there to be found, and that you have to strive for that and work for that. And the notion that it's possible to connect with some[one] else even though they're very different from you.[1]

—Barack Obama

LOOKING AND SEEING

I pass out images of a photograph by Jeff Wall entitled *Invisible Man* and ask students to simply look at the full-color image for a quiet minute. Next, using strategies common to museum and art education, I ask them to describe what they see—not to try to make sense of it, but to just describe the image. "A man sitting." "A black man." "A lot of electrical lights." "A pile of dishes." "A twin-size bed with a quilt." "A suit and dress shoes." The list goes on. As we continue, we begin to shift our descriptions into inferences and hypotheses about what we see. With each detail, the students invent possible scenarios to explain the image. We begin to wonder what is happening in the image to try to piece together a possible story. "Maybe he's in a bunker, hiding from the world," one suggests. "No, I think he's like the Wizard of Oz—he's the great and powerful one behind the curtain," says another. Fifteen minutes pass, and the students collaboratively build on, expand, and debate each other's interpretations. I pause the conversation and turn to Ralph Ellison's prologue to *Invisible Man*, upon which Jeff Wall's photograph is based. Ellison writes: "I am an invisible man. No, I am not a spook like those who haunted Edgar Allan Poe; nor am I one of your Hollywood-movie ectoplasms. I am a man of substance, of flesh and bone, fiber and liquids—and I might even be said to possess a mind. I am invisible, understand, simply because people refuse to see me."[2] And with the addition of this contextual information, our conversation grows personal. One student volunteers how she often feels invisible in an all-male design office because of her gender. Another student says that he increasingly feels a similar invisibility as a black man walking on his own block because more white residents have moved into his childhood neighborhood. A student who is also a high school teacher wonders how often her students feel this invisibility as they shuffle from one classroom to the next.

To be visible, to see and be seen, is often a metaphor for being understood and acknowledged as a person with humanity. But what does it mean to notice something? Are we not seeing and hearing people all day? What then does it mean to look closely and really see the thing, the artwork, the neighborhood, the person in front of you? As images race by us in our media-saturated world, what does it mean to stop and look closely? In clamorous classrooms and multiscreen environments, how do we listen for the solitary sounds of our students' thoughts? And how does that close looking and listening, this noticing of details and nuance, help us understand ourselves and those around us? Critical education scholars who write about culturally responsive and affirming pedagogy speak often about the ways in which authentic awareness of our students—really seeing and hearing them—is an important strategy for building community and moving toward liberatory teaching.[3] As educator Bill Ayers writes, "Teaching is an interactive practice that begins and ends with seeing the student."[4] Focusing on the need to notice, this chapter explores how we can use the arts to teach and learn about the experiences of people in different identity groups or cultures. As literature on multicultural education and folklore studies attest, we must learn to observe how our multiple identities shape our experiences.[5] In doing so, we practice how to move beyond surface observations and assumptions to learn who our students and communities really are—in all of their complexity and contradictions.

As many writers and artists have noted, to notice the world around us is to bear witness to the experiences of people different from us, to acknowledge that we may experience the world in different ways, and those different experiences can enrich our entire worldview. In a world increasingly segregated by race, class, religion, political perspectives, and many other ways in which our identities can be sliced and separated, we need to train ourselves to see and hear the experiences of people who are somehow different from us. Author Jeff Chang writes, "Ending resegregation is about understanding the ways we allow ourselves to stop seeing the humanity of others. It is about learning again to look, and never stopping."[6] Truly seeing each other expands our understandings of our relationships with each other and our awareness of ourselves. Once we start to see the people around us, we cannot ignore them. In acknowledging each other's presence, we honor each other's existence.

Nowhere is this as important as when we are teaching. As one former student, Rafaela noted, "sometimes you see people, but you don't know what's really going on." Social psychologist Joshua Aronson writes about this need to know about our students as individuals: "The experience of not being seen as an individual in the classroom engenders a deep sense of mistrust, separateness, and exclusion."[7] In class, as we discuss the need to notice people, I often start by having the students read psychologist and educator-scholar Beverly Tatum's *Why Are All the Black Kids Sitting Together in the Cafeteria?*, a text whose very title is based on a common observation among educators. Tatum encourages all of us to avoid the silences around race talk and learn with each other; she challenges readers to analyze how their own viewpoints are shaped by their racial identities and how they can better understand and work with people of different races. In my classes, by starting with what we notice about ourselves through reading literature on how to make sense of identity (such as previously mentioned work on levels of identity by Gwyn Kirk and Margo Okazawa-Rey and on privilege by scholars Robin DiAngelo and Özlem Sensoy), educators build a vocabulary to describe what they see in themselves and in our world.[8] We connect these conversations to texts on culturally responsive pedagogy (such as those by educator-scholars Ana María Villegas and Tamara Lucas, Geneva Gay, Wayne Au, Sonia Nieto) as we imagine how to connect what we notice to how we teach.[9] Through texts by art critic Lucy Lippard, we contemplate the importance of home and community, while art educator Kimberly Powell teaches us about art as ethnography and education philosopher Maxine Greene describes art as a tool for "wide awakeness."[10] Throughout these discussions, we consider how to practice noticing by taking cues from artists.

WHAT THE ARTS TEACH US ABOUT NOTICING

We are often taught in our Euro-centric views of art that the classic image of an artist is the portrait or landscape painter. Poised with her brush and palette, this artist dabs paint on a canvas, pauses, squints at her subject, steps back, then adds a touch more paint. Back and forth she moves, from looking intently at the person or place in front of her to trying to capture the image she sees to make it suitable for framing. And while there is much we could critique about this vision, it highlights one of the most important skills of an artist—an ability to notice. In focusing attention on the way light strikes a surface or the shape of an earlobe, artists cultivate the capacity to attend to the details of the world. In doing so, they become adept observers of what they experience. As they turn those observations into works of art, they offer viewers a chance to enter a heightened state of attention with them—to view some slice of the world with focus and awareness.

In the late seventies, artist Mierle Laderman Ukeles began a residency with the New York City Department of Sanitation. Over several years, she interviewed and worked alongside sanitation workers to create several works of art, including *Touch Sanitation*, in which she shook hands with and thanked eighty-five hundred sanitation workers, documenting her interactions through notes and photographs. Her work was lauded for drawing attention to the dignity of the people who truly make a city run. JR, a photographer whose work typically addresses issues of human rights and social justice, completed a project in 2008 focused on the women living in poverty in a neighborhood in Rio de Janeiro, Brazil. Countering media reports of violence and destruction, his large-scale portraits of the eyes and faces of the women who live in this community were plastered on buildings, public stairwells, and residents' homes. Writing about his project, "Women Are Heroes," JR describes his intention to "give a female gaze to both the hill and the favela (neighborhood)" in ways that would highlight the humanity of the people in this community.[11] Developed by two veteran photographers, Peter DiCampo and Austin Merrill, *Everyday Africa* is a social media–based project that crowdsources, curates, and shares images of daily life throughout the continent of Africa. Scenes of family dinners, rock concerts, swimming pools, rugby games, and birthday parties with friends provide viewers with a different story of life in Africa than the scenes of poverty and conflict regularly reported in Western news and textbooks. The quick popularity of these images on Instagram, Facebook, and tumblr have inspired similar offshoots, such as *Everyday Iran*, *Everyday Asia*, and *Everyday Latin America*, that challenge viewers' assumptions about life in other places. Artists such as these demonstrate how we can use art as a tool to help us notice—to practice a stance where we see corners of the world that we do not normally slow down to see or acknowledge.

Drawing inspiration from how artists help us learn to observe the world around us in greater detail, the following activities offer opportunities for students to practice noticing with intentionality. The first activity encourages students to simply spend time looking at and talking about works of art in an effort to hone their observation skills. Along the way, such slowed-down noticing paired with inquiry questions can help students access previously unspoken personal reactions and associations. Turning their attention to these inward reactions, they develop a better understanding of their own biases and assumptions. The second activity moves the practice of noticing from the classroom to the outside world as students create community maps. Just as artists such as Ukeles show us, by leaning outward to observe and intentionally connect with people across difference, we can develop our capacity to notice people for who they are and how their lives intersect with our own.

ACTIVITY 1

To better understand the lenses through which we each view the world, close looking at works of art can help us turn inward to examine our biases, assumptions, and beliefs.

Close Looking at Art

As many arts and museum educators know, the potential for learning by simply spending time looking at and discussing works of art is well documented.[12] Perhaps the simplest activity to facilitate, the strategy of learning to look closely requires little more than time, patience, an interesting work of art, and some good questions. The primary element of this activity is to help educators practice their capacity to observe something for an extended time. Partnered with a few open-ended questions to encourage inquiry into what they are seeing, close looking is exactly as it sounds. A facilitator should first select a work of art to explore through a series of guided questions or prompts. She should then either project this image or pass out high-resolution reproductions of the image to individuals or small groups. The facilitator should encourage participants to quietly examine the work for at least one full, quiet minute to underline the importance of taking time to observe. After participants have had a chance to look quietly, the facilitator should ask participants to simply describe what they notice, ideally without making any immediate interpretations or analyses of the meaning of what they see. These descriptive observations serve several functions: they help us articulate what we are seeing; they help the group collectively focus on details—perhaps pointing to elements others have not yet noticed; they give everyone additional time to look; and they help establish a vocabulary for examining the work of art together. After several participants have had the opportunity to share their initial observations, the facilitator can move into a guided inquiry by asking specific questions about the work of art that enable participants to analyze what they are seeing—how it relates to their own lives and what it can help them consider about the world.

Through careful facilitation, using some of the suggestions in the sidebar "Close Looking," the group can use the work of art as a focus point for increasingly complex conversations about how the work of art can help us turn inward to develop our understandings of who we are in relation to each other. For example, the longer students looked at the details in Jeff Wall's photograph, the more they saw and the more they wondered. Noticing the crumpled quilt on the bed, one student was reminded of her own favorite quilt and recalled who had made it for her. Another student, upon seeing the second record player, began to wonder what kinds of records the figure might be listening to, perhaps using music to calm himself or escape a chaotic world outside the confines of the frame. In looking closely at the image, the students began to see how all the details. Each empty can or faded sepia photograph pinned to the wall helped us deepen our understanding and engagement with the artwork and the possible stories it carried about the specific moment, place, culture, and identity of both the figure in the photograph and the artist who created it. In addition, we were also learning about each other—what one student was drawn to or the memories shared by another classmate. Without leaving our seats, we were expanding our views of ourselves, each other, and the stories captured in the artwork.

Close Looking

Choose a work of art: Research works of art that are relevant to participants. Seek out artwork by artists from local and/or marginalized communities or works that present perspectives from vantage points not often discussed. Allow educators to spend at least a minute simply observing the artwork.

Ask descriptive questions:

- What do you see? Describe what you notice.
- What materials is the work made of?
- What adjectives would you use to describe this work?
- How has the artist composed the work? What kinds of colors, lines, shapes, objects, text, figures, and so on does the artist use?

Ask interpretive questions:

- What decisions might the artist have made about what to include?
- How does this meaning of the work of art change based on your understanding of additional information (such as the title, artist statement, historical or cultural context, critic's analysis, etc.)?

Turn questions inward:

- What does this remind you of?
- What is surprising or puzzling to you about this work?
- What similarities or differences do you notice about your own experiences?

Practical Considerations for Implementation

Choose relevant artworks: If I had one piece of advice that I would underline multiple times, it would be the importance of selecting works of art that are relevant to learners' lives. I do not mean only showing works from a single cultural tradition, but rather identifying works that might connect with students' interests in subject matter, materials, location, place, racial or ethnic identity, or other identity markers. Every educator I spoke with tries to curate a collection of artworks that represent the greatest range of perspectives possible: from different moments in time and locations across the globe; by artists who identify as women, men, transgender, and multiple additional gender identities; and artists of every race, ethnicity, nationality, and religion. They find people who do not call themselves artists but who nevertheless create things. As they do this research, they are also learning— leading to an excellent preparation for conversations with their students. As veteran educator and former student Will noted, this kind of intentionality can make students feel visible: "[It matters] what you show in the classroom:

the artworks on the wall, the artists you show in your slides, the people that you talk about, the music the you play—just making sure you are being ultra-representative, that everyone is represented."

Complicate surface readings: Just as it is imperative that we share artwork from a wide range of historical, cultural, and social perspectives, we must also be wary of essentializing those artists and artworks as simply tied to one identifier. Jasmin, a former student in the class, describes one of the most common examples of this pitfall: "If you pick a particular piece of artwork and feel like that piece of artwork is representative to a whole entire group of people, [that is] just overgeneralizing." She offers a very common example: "It is like saying, 'So we're going to do kente cloth everything for February because it's Black History Month!' That could go really bad, especially if you have no idea what kente cloth is for and why people use it." Not only does this move frame kente cloth as only related to black history—thereby essentializing it as if it has no other possible interpretations, uses, meaning, or relevancy to learners' lives—but it also limits learners' possible connections to the artwork. Jasmin continues, "Is your purpose to show people, 'Hey! I'm not racist so I'm gonna just show art from black people today 'cause I'm not black' or is it because you really feel like these particular pieces of artwork speak to our higher technical or social leaning goals. There has to be a connection to a grander [learning] goal, not just because 'kente' means black history. It has to be more." When we choose artwork based *only* on its capacity to teach about identity, we risk doing more harm by limiting the opportunities for multiple interpretations and intersectional analyses of why the artwork might have different meanings for each of us. To avoid this, educators can research multiple perspectives and potential connections about the works of art they select.[13]

Provide time and direction to focus: By taking time to look at a work of art before even starting to talk about it and then spending upward of ten or even thirty minutes in a guided conversation about the work, learners have a chance to hone their ability to observe. Educators can encourage learners to slow down by providing prompts about what to look at or additional contextual information about the artists or work of art. For example, we might direct learners to focus on the postures of figures in an image or the color palette the artist employed. Writing or drawing prompts that ask learners to draw or write down what they see can also slow our impulses to look quickly.

Ask inquiry questions: Open-ended questions that encourage analytic and imaginative thinking are the keys to successfully facilitating a conversation about a work of art. This is the opportunity to try all the variations of what, when, who, where, why, and how. That said, a few basic initial questions can launch any conversation about art: "What do you see here?" "What makes you say that?" "Why might that matter?" The first question encourages viewers to practice naming what they see. The second question helps them support their observations with some kind of evidence. And the third question pushes them to think about the meaning of the work—perhaps to them personally, to the conversation at hand, or to society itself. I have found that iterations of this third question are what help propel conversations about identity. To do this, educators should use the full spectrum of questioning and discussion strategies, from analyzing comparisons and identifying relevant connections, to fostering debates and imagining alternative interpretations.[14]

ACTIVITY 2

Moving from looking and talking about works of art to creating their own can help students lean outward as they practice intentionally noticing.

Community Mapping

For centuries, artists have used maps to tell stories and illustrate ideas about places and people. From the scientifically detailed to the wildly imaginative, maps communicate the relationships between things—be they physical spaces, remembered landscapes, modes of movement, or even pathways of communication. We consult maps on a near-daily basis: public transportation maps, GPS devices, floor plans of office buildings, color-coded diagrams of the brain or our nervous system, grocery store directional signs, and weather radar screens. Each map conveys meaning beyond the surface imagery through our associations with lines, relationships between objects, previous experience, and common assumptions. For example, when we watch a dark-red shape pass over the green shape labeled with our hometown's name on a weather map, we know to reach for an umbrella on our way out the door. In this way, maps use symbols to tell us stories about the world around us. To create a map, then, is to tell a particular story about a place or an idea.

When I ask students to create a map of a community they are getting to know, I am asking them to practice noticing and to tell me a story about what they see (see the sidebar "Community Mapping" for suggestions on initiating this activity). Designing a map requires that we stop to observe the world around us, to see how one road connects to another or where the dairy products are in relation to the vegetables or how lifting one finger activates one specific part of our brains. In other words, it forces us to see how objects, places, and people interact, to describe the relationships between them. Because of this, it is the ideal tool for encouraging us to examine the world and identify how the different elements connect, intersect, and refract. In doing so, we must learn to watch closely and listen carefully to what may have previously felt like second nature. Through a process of learning to notice closely and listen carefully to a community outside their usual social spheres, students create visual representations of the physical and/or social space of a community.

Examples of past community maps include both realistic street maps as well as abstract maps of the relationships, movement, or other conceptual aspect of a group of people. Created with photographs, line drawings, embroidery, video, or any local materials the students have collected in their explorations, these maps become useful tools for analyzing both what we see in communities outside our own and what we are more inclined to be looking for. For students interested in building relationships with people in a community tied to a physical location, such as Hunts Point in the Bronx, their particular school community, or a senior center, the prompt to make a map may feel rather straightforward. We are comfortable with street maps and building plans that point to how people move through space, the key landmarks, and the representation of our built environment. For those students who are eager to connect with people in less physically delineated communities, such as the community of aspiring actors or people who are in transitional housing, the task of mapmaking poses a different challenge. In this case, students must consider how people within these communities think about their connection to the city in the first place. Not surprisingly, as one student learned, aspiring actors were more likely to build connections to the cafés, restaurants, housing, and neighborhoods closest to the theater district. Meanwhile, the student trying to better understand what it means to rely on transitional housing found that the people she spoke to paid attention to issues of safety and ease of access to public transportation when they navigated the city. Another student who was hoping to better know her own neighbors sought to create a map that depicted how the Nigerian immigrants she met talked about their connections both to New York City and to their home country. The task of creating a map stretches participants to notice relationships that they had not previously tended to in their daily lives.

Community Mapping

Consider visible interactions: Direct students to pay attention to how the community of people whom they are getting to know interacts with social and physical space: how do people talk about, mark, and move through space?

Contemplate invisible relationships: Think beyond the physicality of the city so that students pay attention to how people describe their relationships to each other, to places, and to ideas that have meaning for them.

Analyze observations: Ask students to describe the evidence they are relying on as they make their observations; in other words, how do we make sense of what we notice? What do our observations tell us about our own values and perspectives? (For example, does a self-proclaimed foodie pay more attention to the restaurants in a neighborhood?)

Match the map materials to the stories: Choose art materials and methods that align with the stories students want to tell about their observations. If one is documenting invisible relationships between various members of a community, perhaps abstract imagery is more useful. If one is focused on the ways in which people congregate in various informal settings, perhaps realistic imagery is most appropriate.

Practical Considerations for Implementation

Go outside: You can't make a map using Google, even though it is tempting to try. Nearly every time I assign the community map, someone asks if they really need to go outside physically to research their map. Given the ease of the internet, I fear far too often that this is how we try to get to know each other and our students. We read articles, watch movies, and might even use Google's map function to explore a neighborhood. Yet, we all know that how we are depicted as individuals (in our social media profiles) and communities (in news reports, blog posts, commentaries) is rarely ever a complete or even true representation. To build real, nuanced understandings of each other, we need to be present in person. This means spending time physically with people to observe the sights, sounds, smells, and emotions of how we interact with each other, how we move, react, and engage (or don't) with our various contexts. To really notice, we need to turn off our laptops and phones and step outside.

In being physically present with people, we can also practice seeing people as full, complex humans worthy of dignity and respect, rather than subjects to study. As I wrote earlier, this move parallels the potential of "othering" a person instead of seeing him or her as simply another person who has different life experiences and perspectives. While art can often help us better understand the complexity of people, it can often be used to oversimplify people's experiences and turn them into objects for study. Writing about how photography can desensitize us to the experiences of trauma and war, Susan Sontag warns that "[t]o photograph people is to violate them as they never see themselves, by having knowledge of them they can never have; it turns people into objects that can be symbolically possessed."[15] When creating maps or visual documents of people, we must be ever wary that we resist objectifying people in the process. This is why it is particularly important to have face-to-face encounters with people, to go out in the world to actually share physical space with people. It is far easier to objectify people when we view them through a lens—whether of a camera or the internet. Once we step into our own vulnerability to meet people for who they are—in all of their complexity and humanness—we are far less likely to think of them as objects.

Consider the stories our observations tell: The maps that the students have created over the years stretch from detailed renderings of every storefront on a specific block (complete with signage, awnings, and store hours), to hand-embroidered abstract lines on paper depicting the very real challenge of even trying to record a community. As we discuss these maps in class, we realize that not only are the maps telling us stories about the communities we are getting to know, but they are also telling us stories about ourselves—what we gravitate toward, what makes us excited or nervous, and how we often record the elements of a community that we ourselves value. This critical reflection is imperative to move the mapping beyond surface observations. While there are many ways to encourage critical analyses of their maps, I typically pose a series of questions to help focus students' looking: What do you notice about how people interact with space? With each other? What places, landmarks, or paths appear important? What's missing? What patterns do you notice? How do you know? Questions such as these encourage mapmakers to pause to think about what they are seeing and to consider how their own lenses shape that view.

Look for nuance and complexity: One of the major risks in asking students to create visual maps of a community is the potential for generalizations. Part of making a map often requires the mapmaker to distill large amounts of information into a simple illustration or representation. While it is one thing to use a symbol of a tree to signify a forest on a map, it is another to turn observations about communities of people into simplified imagery. This kind of thinking can lead participants to reinforce preexisting assumptions or even foster new ones. It can be tempting to leap for generalizations when one is just starting to get to know a group of people for the first time. Even well-intentioned ones—"everyone was out talking on their stoops; they must be a close-knit group"—do harm in that they hide the diverse range of experiences within communities. Once we lock onto these generalizations, they can prevent us from seeing the nuances and complexities among people. While the tendency to generalize is common, we can help educators avoid the damage of generalizing by continually reminding ourselves that such generalities obscure the multifaceted realities of identity. Harkening back to our terms of engagement, I remind educators that identity is constantly shifting, layered, and contextual, often in ways that we cannot readily see on the surface. Critical questions as educators reflect on their maps can help them resist leaping to conclusions based on their initial observations.

Practice humility: Creating a community map is as much about understanding ourselves as the community we are mapping. When we keep the focus on our own growth, it helps us learn to notice and listen to our own biases, assumptions, and understandings. To do this, participants must approach their mapmaking with humility and a desire to learn about themselves. I encourage them to continually ask themselves questions about their own intentions, such as: Why am I stepping out of my comfort zone? What do

I hope to gain? What am I willing to give? In remembering that we are all in a constant state of growth, learners are more likely to bring a sense of humility and openness to their community interactions.

Learning to Notice

In interviews with alumni from my classes, some former students reflected vividly on the ways in which they developed a more nuanced capacity to notice the people and communities they regularly interact with as well as their own biases, values, and assumptions. Talking about who we are and how we relate to other people can be complicated, emotional, and sometimes scary, yet it is the only way we can learn to better connect across difference. By practicing our ability to notice our world and our reactions within it, we can create stronger tools to build relationships with people from different backgrounds. Both the close-looking and community-mapping activities provide a chance to practice a noticing stance: closely looking enables students to turn inward as they learn to notice what they see, while community mapping challenges students to lean outward to learn through their interactions with people in real life. Reflections from former students highlight the ways in which encounters with looking at and making art deepened their capacity to notice.

Turning Inward

Through looking closely at works of art, students practiced the all-too-rare task of publicly talking about concepts of identity. In doing so, they broke the prevalent silences around talking about who we are and the associated powers and privileges of our identities, they engaged with artwork made by artists from different cultural backgrounds, and they began to see their own lenses through which they view the world.

Artworks as conversation starters: Whenever I share works of art with students and ask them to discuss what they see, we quickly end up talking about concepts of identity. Students raise questions about what they see and what an artist might be trying to convey. They wonder aloud about possible interpretations of a figure's skin color, class, religion, gender, occupation, purpose, values, and beliefs. They invent stories and share them openly. They describe personal connections to the artwork. In other words, they just start talking. The arts can surface ideas that we can't easily talk about by making them visual and outside ourselves. Suddenly, we're not talking directly to each other about our views of identity, but instead we're talking together about a third object—the artwork—in front of us. Jane, an art teacher at an all-girls high school, describes this process: "I think through looking at art we become a participant of it. We're able to have a conversation with it and in having the conversation with the work of art . . . you kind of establish this dialogue." Pausing, Jane remembers an article she once read: "This journalist said these paintings are my old friends. And so I think looking at artwork, we can have this happy conversation." In this way, as Jane says, we "take the looking to each other."

When works of art act as third-party "friends" to our conversations about complex ideas such as race, class, gender, religion, and our many other intersecting identities, they play the role of the conversation starter and focal point. Through their discussions about their interpretations of a work of art, viewers can describe their ideas to or about the work of art rather than to or about a classmate or colleague. In this way, the works of art can also diffuse the emotions that often arise when we talk about our identities enough to create a space to listen to and notice each other's ideas.

Gateway to other perspectives: When viewing artwork in the context of teaching identity, community, and culture, educators can spark discussions that challenge or reaffirm the message or interpretation of the artwork. High school teacher Jasmin points to the many ways in which "looking at the artwork of another person is like peeking into their personal point of view of something. Just talking about a piece of artwork alone will give a person hints as to 'what do they fear?' 'What are their stereotypes?' What they don't know and what they do know.'" These critical questions support our capacity to notice perspectives different than our own.

High school art teacher Kendra reflected on her own experience viewing Lalla Essaydi's photographs of modern Egyptian women on whom she has inscribed Islamic texts in henna: "I think in her pictures she was actually—because it was from her culture—I think she was reflecting on her experiences . . . so she was able to put a piece of herself in the piece." In the context of closely looking at Essaydi's work, the class discussed the artist's personal statement: "In my art, I wish to present myself through multiple lenses—as artist, as Moroccan, as Saudi, as traditionalist, as Liberal, as Muslim. In short, I invite the viewer to resist stereotypes."[16] Both Kendra and the artist highlight how looking at works of art can provide opportunities for viewers to reflect on cultures, value systems, and ways of being quite different than their own. Noticing these new perspectives, just as Kendra did, expands each viewer's understanding of not only another person's experiences, but also one's own.

Identifying our own lenses: When we take the time to look closely at and collectively discuss works of art, it's often hard to avoid seeing something of ourselves. We are often drawn to the parts of an image that relate to our own lives—the colors or sounds that speak to us, the imagery that reminds us of something we've experienced before, the subject matter that echoes elements of our own life. Even if the work seems to be as far from our lives as possible, once we start discussing it with other people, we often see additional meanings and interpretations. We see ourselves in the reflections that artists provide in their work. And often, in those new reflections, we start to understand our own perspectives better. As Jackie, a former student, describes her own teaching, she discusses the ways in which artists model being more open about our own identities: "[Even] if we are not interested in talking about our own identity, the artist has put themselves out there and we can talk about *their* identity and then, because we are talking about them, we can relate it to ourselves."

When we talk about the Jeff Wall image, we always start by discussing the images in front of us. As I described earlier, we talk about the details and potential meanings of the work. However, every time I have taught from this image, someone soon mentions what visibility means to them, how they have felt visible or invisible. Someone else always wonders aloud about the times they might have not seen someone. From there, we can talk about the blind spots and lenses we each bring to our analysis of the work. In asking them why they might have these experiences, they talk about their own layered identities. This happens not just with Jeff Wall's *Invisible Man* photograph, but with nearly every image that I teach from. We cannot look at a work and discuss it without seeing it through our own lenses. The trick is helping each other to identify what those lenses are.

Leaning Outward

As we share and reflect on the community maps, students often recount their surprise at what they've noticed about another community—and about themselves. By leaning out of their comfort zones to meet people outside their typical social circles, their understanding of themselves and others inevitably expands. As students start to see buildings, streets, and abstract connections through new lenses, their views of how they observe their world are heightened.

Noticing new connections: Often, students in my classes choose to create maps about physical neighborhoods following conventional formats of street maps. They typically note the landmarks that stand out to them, the names of stores and parks, religious centers, and other visible sites. As they discuss these maps, they inevitably remark on the details they had never noticed before—even when documenting their own neighborhoods. Focusing attention on the Pakistani community in her own neighborhood, for example, one student realized that a Pakistani community center was on her own block. Even though it was on her route to the subway, she had never noticed it before. Likewise, another student, a self-declared nonreligious person, created a visual map of all of the churches in his neighborhood after he started paying closer attention to the buildings and spaces in his own backyard. Reflecting on his map, he was shocked not only at how many churches he had found—of various sizes and denominations—but at how he had hardly seen them before the challenge to look more closely.

Through what several students described as "slow looking," the task of creating a visual map requires them to observe with intentionality. By training themselves to pay attention to the details they so often miss, the students practiced attending to patterns, connections, and relationships between people that they otherwise would have overlooked. Elle reflected on her own "noticings" in the neighborhood she had lived in for almost three years:

> I know a couple of my neighbors pretty well, but it was just like, slowing down, and reading the signs, especially in Harlem, there's so many. There's so much old beautiful signage that you don't necessarily see . . . it was cool to just slow down and think about what street I walk down and do I always walk down the same side of the street or do I go on the other side? . . . What happens if I go across the street and go on the other side? Do I notice other things? So it was a cool way to pay attention to my surroundings . . . taking in the experience of all the senses and not just eyesight but the idea of taste and feelings.

As Elle highlights, this kind of intentional looking takes practice and focus.

Once students start noticing their environments more closely, they also analyze what they see. Describing her experience creating a map of her own neighborhood, Jackie noted that "[t]he community map made me look at my community that I chose, my neighborhood, in different ways; like looking at a map, looking for a history of the place or looking in detail—[I came to see] the place in a different way." She continued, "That just made me look at every part of it equally, like putting it all on the same page, literally putting everything on the same page, because my experience of [the neighborhood] is usually that my street is the most important, I go here the most, so it's like the biggest place in my mind. But then if I insert all these other stores or these other streets and they're all equal, what happens?" In mapmaking, the primary challenge is to figure out how to visualize the relationships between components. Jackie's question highlights the kinds of questions that can arise when we start to really notice not just the immediate details of our worlds, but also how they fit together.

Visualizing assumptions and connections: Moving from becoming astute observers of their communities, students are then tasked with translating those observations into a visual document of what they notice. Whether abstract or realistic, these maps contain important information not just about the people and places students are getting to know, but perhaps more importantly, these maps tell stories about their creators. To create a map, mapmakers choose what to include and what to leave out. They select what they think is critical information to share. They choose the images, colors, and formats to convey that information. They determine the relationships between each component. In this way, creating a work of art offers students an opportunity to make public their (seemingly) private perspectives. The artwork is then a tool for showing us what we notice—and what we miss— when we observe the world. We can hold up these visual documents of what we have seen, heard, noticed, smelled, and felt as mirrors to help us see our own assumptions about and connections to people we might not have thought about previously.

When Denise, a former student who now teaches elementary school, set out to learn more about her own school community, she didn't think she had many assumptions about the predominantly white, affluent, private school community in which she worked. Although she was aware that her own life experience as a black woman from a less wealthy part of New York City was different from the experiences of her students, she was surprised when she publicly shared her map with classmates and began to see her own assumptions embedded in her map. She and I later discussed this realization: "I feel like I had, I put a lot of my assumptions in there. It's also factual, but the things I chose to include were my assumptions of them." I asked her when she became aware of those assumptions, and she replied, "I think when we did that gallery walk [activity to view everyone's maps] and people wrote comments on it. I realized that I was sort of putting them [members of my school community] in a box because my classmates were like, 'Oh this is very like rich people or very white.' There was a New York Sports Club and a Starbucks—I think the things I chose to add were sort of, I guess subconsciously, assumptions I had about [the families who attend my school]." Denise expressed surprise at this realization: "[I]t's like, oh, I didn't realize that's what I did. That's exactly what I did."

As Denise and I discuss this moment, she expands on why the act of making and sharing her map helped her see her assumptions: "I think because there's no explanation behind it, it's just pictures and you get to, you just notice what you notice. It's just an open-ended thing, you get to see something and you get to make meaning in your own way. It was fun to make that map . . . that seems to be an important element of it too, right? Here we are talking about things like identity, you know heavy things right and then . . . it can be fun." Caught up in the fun of making a map—of translating what they noticed in their community into a work of art—many students are more likely to share their initial reactions. Whereas in an explicit conversation about identity, many students might hide their assumptions out of fear of harming someone or sounding hurtful, through their artwork, they are often less inhibited. This can allow for an honest assessment of one's initial reactions and previously unsurfaced biases. Creating a map and then sharing it with a critical audience can help us better understand how what we notice tells us who we are.

Sharing space with people: Although it sounds simple, one of the reasons why the task of creating a visual map of getting to know a community is useful is that it forces students to share space with people with whom they may not typically interact. As anyone who has ever been invited to a friend's home knows, the act of entering someone else's space is an act of intimacy. You see how they arrange their lives, what objects (if any) they possess and display, what foods they prepare, how they move when they're most comfortable, where they sleep, what they cherish. This is why going home to meet a new loved one's family is such a big deal. Our spaces tell stories about who we are, how we came to be this way, and what we hope to become. And that's not all. We also learn about ourselves when we stop by a neighbor's house and see that their furniture arrangement and photo displays are entirely different from those in our own homes. When we return home, we see our own decorating choices through new eyes.

As part of their community engagement project, I also require students to attend a public event within the community they are getting to know. This task inevitably strikes fear in many students. Together, we revisit our terms of engagement and discuss what they can learn by leaning into the discomfort they feel about entering the public space of another community. With humility, they research an event—a local festival, public talk, religious service, community meeting, scheduled meet-up, or special program—to share space with members of the community with whom they hope to connect. And they go—even when it feels awkward.

Andy, a white student who described himself as unaffiliated with any religion, ended up attending a church service for Chinese Americans in an effort to deepen his understandings of those from Brooklyn's Chinatown community. While he felt comfortable entering the building and finding a seat, that comfort shifted as he started to talk with the people around him: "I think it was awkward partly because in the church, they were interested in bringing their reasons for being there to me, and I had reasons for being there that were really different from that—like [my reasons] were not about Jesus! And so to try to be totally respectful of that and not push that away like, 'No you don't get to try to interest me in Jesus, I only get to find out about you for my school project!'" Sharing space, Andy learned, was about a kind of reciprocal learning. As he put it, "There had to be some give-and-take there." This kind of negotiation is a key point of learning for many students who come to understand that when they enter someone else's space, they must respect the codes, dignity, and humanity of the community's "home." Once Andy leaned into the discomfort of being in a space with someone different, he noticed "generosity" from those he encountered as he started talking with people. By the end, despite his reticence to engage in conversations about religion, he embraced an attitude of "alright I'm gonna hear you out about this other thing" that opened up avenues of communication with those he met.

Almost every student who attends a public event in an effort to share space with people outside their usual networks describes a sense of anxiety at broaching the social barriers that often keep groups of people segregated. Yet, nearly everyone leaves with a new awareness of themselves and the people with whom they are hoping to connect. Reflecting on her experience attending a community event in her predominantly black neighborhood, Stefanie, who is white, describes the sense of nervousness she felt: "I went to this big street festival where there were vendors selling like food and crafts and music performances . . . being one of the only white people there definitely felt educational I guess. Because it was just striking, like I definitely feel a little bit uncomfortable and just kind of more aware of everything that I'm doing . . . it's like I'm feeling very aware of where I'm standing, and how I'm interacting with people, and I want to make sure to be as polite and smiling as possible and just hyper-aware of everything I was doing." She goes on to describe how this experience forced her to think about her own identity: "And then the idea [that] that's the daily experience of most people who aren't white . . . I'm trying to think about my own identity."

Like Stefanie, many students describe a sense of relief after sharing space with people they might often (consciously or not) avoid. They return to our discussions with animated stories about how "it wasn't that bad!" And how they met people who were kind, welcoming, and warm. Everyone describes how their initial assumptions and expectations were way off. And this part is key because learning how to acknowledge those assumptions, move through them to share space with people, and then to let those assumptions fade is a critical tool for educators. Certainly, our own young learners have some of the same hesitations about entering the space we have created our own classrooms—spaces that are crafted out of our own values, priorities, and needs. If we can nurture our ability to listen for and notice those hesitations, we can find ways to work through them—to perhaps even create some new mutually shared space with our students. Thinking back on his experience in the church, Andy related his reactions to his own teaching: "I think in the church, not feeling like I shouldn't be there, or that somehow I was doing something that was messing with their space, or somehow invading; but it's good for people to cross those boundaries. And if I come with a lot of, a lot of, I wanna say love, like you know, positivity and respect, and I'm actually trying to be less ignorant about you here. I think if you can do that, if you can be okay with who you are in the situation, that helps. And then there's space to have conversations."

Reflecting on how he started building trust with his neighborhood's school community, novice educator Chris described advice he had once received: "Someone said this to me a long time ago, something to the effect that people trust you in as much as they can see you—like see who you are and what you're about. I've really taken that to heart 'cause I think it's really true." To see people for who they are—to really listen and notice people—is no easy task. It takes patience, focus, and practice. Yet, it's possible that in "really listening [to people] and taking them in in ways that allow them to be themselves," we can nurture connections with each other. Chris continued, "I think when you're extending yourself across to connect with people that do not share your same identities, and your same background—[they] don't even look like you, or dress like you—I think it's really important that you listen, be vulnerable, show the biggest range of who you are—through your emotions, through your mind, and the way you carry yourself physically—as you can, so they can see you. Because I think that creates safety for a lot of people." That safety and the trust that accompanies it, Chris muses, is a tool to help us really see—to notice—each other across some of the social and cultural barriers that divide us.

CHAPTER 3

Wondering Stance

I don't write out of what I know; I write out of what I wonder. I think most artists create art in order to explore, not to give the answers. Poetry and art are not about answers to me; they are about questions.

—Lucille Clifton[1]

WALK (AND DRAW) THE LINE

After the first few weeks of class, we have established a sense of community that results in much before-class chatter, as people share updates about their community projects, teaching, or weekend plans. Because of this, the silence I suddenly request can feel awkward as I ask everyone to form a straight line, shoulder to shoulder, in the middle of an empty room. I explain that I will read aloud a series of statements about different life experiences, along with directions to take a small step either forward or backward. Everyone is to stay focused on their own steps; no one is required to move unless they feel ready to do so. I slowly read the statements: "If English is your first language, take one step forward." "If one or both of your parents have a college degree, take a step forward." "If you can easily find Band-Aids designed to blend in with or match your skin tone, take one step forward." "If you studied the culture of your ancestors in school, take one step forward." "If your family has ever left your homeland or entered another country not of your own free will, take a step back." (Sometimes the statements cause someone to knowingly shake their head.) "If you would never think twice about calling the police when trouble occurs, take one step forward." (Sometimes there is an audible sigh.) "If your family has health insurance, take a step forward." "If you can show affection for your romantic partner in public without fear of ridicule or violence, move ahead one step." (Sometimes many people move forward at once.) "If you were ever discouraged from an activity because of race, class, ethnicity, gender, disability, or sexual orientation, take a step back." "If you constantly feel unsafe walking alone at night, back one step."

As I read each statement from this common diversity training activity, students spread apart from the original center line. The classmates they had aligned with at first are now several feet ahead or behind them. Everyone looks forward; only those in the back can see everyone else in front. Carefully, I survey the students' faces. Some seem pained, others resigned. Often, someone blinks back tears. When I finish reading the statements, I ask everyone to pause for a moment and notice their own reactions. I encourage them to look around. I remind them not to say a word, as everyone returns to their seats.

Still holding their quiet reflection, I pass out sheets of paper and drawing pencils. I ask them to consider the many ways a simple line can represent an idea or an emotion. I tell them to think about the experience of the activity and to draw a line that conveys their thoughts. Almost everyone starts immediately. Some actually draw with a ferocity that is almost audible—creating a deep, thick line. For others, the line is fainter, more intimate, almost lacelike. Once everyone is finished, we hang up their drawings for everyone to see and then step back to analyze the images.

Every time I lead this line-walking and line-making activity, there are always multiple zigzags (some ending up and others plummeting to the bottom of the page); at least one thick, straight, horizontal line; and several spirals of varying boldness. Using their lines as descriptors, students discuss their experiences taking steps forward and backward. Pointing to a diagonal line, one student talks about how the activity left her feeling ashamed for her privilege, a comment that prompts another student to say that she felt a surprising sense of pride at where she stood. Throughout our conversation, students refer to the lines they have drawn to narrate their reactions. As they do, they notice connections between their lines. The students who have drawn heavy, dark lines ask each other about their experiences. Those with totally unique patterns—perhaps a dashed line or a knot of lines—spark curiosity, as students question the potential meanings. Someone points to a single circle and wonders aloud what the artist was thinking, prompting a conversation about possible interpretations. Another student looks at the range of lines and suggests that they connect them all, wondering if, in doing so, their collective lines will tell a different kind of story about the experience.

As we talk, students weave in their reflections on walking the lines of their privilege in a public forum. They describe how creating the lines gave them a chance to collect their thoughts as they imagined how to translate experiences into works of art. As they do, they wonder about how their classmates felt and how their own students might also experience the world. Looking closely at the collected lines on the wall—faint or dramatic, clear or tangled—they have a visible document of their reflections. Despite the emotion of the activity, students use the lines to ask questions, sometimes directly to each other and sometimes about the systems of socialization that have determined which steps we take forward or backward. The forced silence is broken.

R R R

As any educator can confirm, a good question can be the key to unlocking most forms of silence. From the quiet that comes from not knowing something to the reticence that comes from not wanting to engage in a topic, a thoughtful question can be the motivator to shift from clammed up to curious. As education philosopher Maxine Greene wrote, the task of educators is to "provoke learners to pose their own questions, to teach themselves . . . to name their worlds . . . they have to question why."[2] Good questions encourage us to wonder—to reflect on what we know and what might be. In thinking about identity, a caring question can be just what we need to force us out of our comfort zones to consider who we are in relation to each other. Such wondering is thus a call to participate in the pursuit of knowledge—a way of instigating learning.

When educators exercise their capacity to wonder with students, they help learners build analytic lenses through which they can view the world. As we talk about the shifting, contextual, and layered nature of who we are, this ability to wonder about nuance, ambiguity, and multiplicity is incredibly important. When students spend time looking at each other's drawings in response to the "walk the line" activity, they wonder and ask questions about not only their own reactions, but also those of the people around them. In doing so, they loosen a grip on their previously held beliefs as they allow for new ideas, perspectives, and reactions to sneak in. Suddenly, things might not be as simple as they had once seemed. Other explanations might exist. Perhaps we are not who we thought we were; nor is our neighbor. Wondering becomes a tool for dislodging the stubbornly strong ideas we have been taught about ourselves, our students, and our communities.

To wonder about who each of us is in the world is to embrace the idea that our current realities are not set in stone. Instead, we can reimagine what we have been taught about ourselves and each other. Such wondering activates a form of caring curiosity that enables us to rethink our preestablished ideas. "Curiosity," as social psychologist Joshua Aronson reminds us, "is the diametrical opposite of stereotyping and prejudice."[3] To practice the stance of someone who wonders is to admit that we can reinvent the social structures that tell us how to behave, who to talk to, who to avoid, and with whom we belong. In other words, this stance grants us the tools to scrutinize the social and cultural barriers that often divide us, to seek out the weak spots, and to wonder who we might be if we step outside, across, or through those barriers.

As we wonder about who each of us is in relation to another, we consult theoretical texts about power, such as educator-scholar Paulo Freire's *Pedagogy of the Oppressed* and practitioner-oriented scholarship about the power dynamics associated with socially constructed categories of race, gender, class, nationality, and ability.[4] Reading art critic Lucy Lippard's views on the concept of home remind us of the importance of place and community in people's lives, while school administrator Grant Kashatok and educator-scholar Leisy Wyman teach us about "triangulating teachers," who "seek constantly to learn about communities, always resisting quick blanket explanations for local practices."[5] We consider lessons from ethnography that highlight how attentive, genuine, and respectful research about people's lives can help us learn about perspectives different from our own.[6] And finally, we read poetry and prose by Audre Lorde, Claudia Rankine, Sherman Alexie, Adrienne Rich, and others as we examine how the arts encourage a kind of wondering necessary to connect with people.

WHAT THE ARTS TEACH US ABOUT WONDERING

What if? This question is at the root of all art making. What if I could convey joy in the curve of a line? What if a character swerved onto a different path? What if dissonant sounds blended? What if this stone were really a body? Or vice versa? To create a work of art is to ask a question and to wonder about the potential answers. Ask any artists, any people who create things, and they will tell you that they spend time wondering. They wonder about how different materials function or how sounds might merge. They wonder about the connections between ideas and how they might convey those. They wonder about the potential for new worlds and how they might create them. This wondering and questioning continues throughout their production—in fact, it doesn't actually stop. After creating a work, artists have already started asking the next question.

In addition to providing the initial start for a work of art, questions—and the wondering they inspire—serve an additional purpose: they open doors to new understandings about ourselves and the world around us. In asking questions, artists explore the dimensions of what it means to be human. As they do, they uncover hidden truths and unexpected realities about themselves and their relationships with the people around them. In one multiyear project titled *American Alphabets*, photographer Wendy Ewald asked young people from similar cultural communities to identify a word that is meaningful to them. She then worked with each young person to compose an image depicting that word—sometimes using props or gestures, other times having the young people manipulate the photograph once it was taken. She has created visual alphabets with Spanish-speaking children of immigrant farm workers, African American children in Cleveland, white girls in a private academy, and Arabic-speaking middle schoolers whose families moved to New York City from Egypt, Jordan, Algeria, Morocco, and Lebanon. Asked to consider words that resonate for them, students in the project identified words that connect to their own identities: words such as talk, nappy, queen, insecure, *'ima* (blind), *kitab* (book), *voltear* (to turn), *nervosa* (nervous). The final visual alphabets are displayed for public audiences, and as Ewald writes, "Taken as a whole, their lists of words amounted to a kind of cultural self-portrait."[7] Viewing (and likely creating) these *American Alphabets* forces one to reconsider how language shapes and is shaped by who each of us is.

Ewald's intimate alphabet project highlights how making and looking at art can help us question and wonder about who we are, what we find meaningful, and how that might align with or differ from what others find important. In addition to this kind of personal reflection, interactions with art can also stretch our capacity to reconsider the social structures that define and often limit who we are. Such wondering can help us flex our imaginations, enabling us, as Greene writes, to look "beyond the boundary where the backyard ends or the road narrows, diminishing out of sight."[8] In other words, we can begin to see new ways of being. For many artists, this is one of their primary tasks—to help us wonder what might be possible.

With a stack of preprinted stickers in the shape and style of a "Hello, my name is" nametag, artist Candy Chang's *I Wish This Was* project prompted community members in New Orleans to fill in the blank and reenvision their neighborhoods. The easy-to-remove vinyl stickers pose a provocative question to passersby, who are encouraged to wonder what might be possible. Writing about her work, she recalls responses ranging from "the functional to the poetic: I wish this was . . . a butcher shop, a community garden, a place to sit and talk, a city without theft, your dream, Heaven."[9] Working in a similar vein, environmental artist Eve Mosher designed a digital fill-in-the-blank arrow emblazoned with the words "Insert _____ here." Like Chang, Mosher urges viewers to wonder what might be missing in their communities. Mosher encourages people to print the green arrows themselves, add their thoughts, and then photograph the sign in context. She shares the images on her website. Someone writes in "a bike rack" and affixes the arrow to a signpost. Someone else simply scrawls "park" and tapes the sign to a chained fence. As people participate in both Chang's and Mosher's projects, they are asked to question the realities in front of them and to wonder just what might be.

As we try to build relationships across social divisions, the need for a rigorous imagination is real. Artists provide important counternarratives to the dominant stories we are told about each other. In doing so, they spur us to develop our wondering stances as we critically analyze how we connect (or not) with those around us. To practice this kind of wondering with students, I facilitate two activities that seek to hone their capacity to question their own perspectives and to wonder about the lives of people different from them. The first activity asks students to create comics about specific scenarios that highlight common misconceptions about identity. Creating imagery to accompany stories encourages students to turn inward to reflect on their own biases as they design short graphic stories of real events. The second activity encourages students to consider the perspectives of another person as they create a portrait of a conversation they have had with someone different from them. The conversation portraits nudge students to lean outward from their typical modes of interaction with people to listen attentively and wonder with compassionate curiosity about another person's life. Pairing both inward reflection with outward action enables students to nurture a wondering stance that is at once personal and social.

ACTIVITY 1

To prompt students to wonder more critically about how identity shapes their own lived experience, I begin with both an art form and real-life scenarios that are often very familiar to students.

Scenario Comics

Comics—also referred to as sequential art or graphic novels—are, at their most basic, a mix of text and image used to tell a story. Typically, the images in comics are somewhat simplified, abstracted, or distilled to iconography. In this way, comic artists can use even very basic drawings to convey complex ideas through careful cropping, symbols, and the composition of text and imagery. (Though it should also be noted that there are many comic artists or graphic novelists who are accomplished realistic illustrators creating astoundingly complicated images.) This ability to make accessible images is part of the unique strength of the comic form. As comic artist and scholar Scott McCloud writes, "[W]hen you look at a photo or realistic drawing of a face, you see it as the face of *another*. But when you enter the world of the *cartoon*, you see yourself."[10] Comics encourage us to step into the characters depicted on the page and to enter imagined worlds.

Because of how they invite readers into the story, comics serve as a useful medium for fostering analytic thinking about identity.[11] In class, I typically assign several academic texts to provide students with theoretical lenses through which they can examine their own identities. We spend a significant amount of time discussing the five aspects of a "culture of power" in Lisa Delpit's "The Silenced Dialogue: Power and Pedagogy in Educating Other People's Children."[12] Her potent and useful descriptions of power as it relates to identity can be challenging for students to process. To help them question how power intersects with their multiple identities, particularly as educators, I ask the students to create a comic of a moment in which identity-related power played out in their teaching. Sometimes these are moments when race- or gender-based assumptions have resulted in obvious discrimination (such as name-calling or hiring discrimination); at other times, the moments are more subtly tied to the cultural biases or blind spots we each have (such as teaching texts from only one worldview or underestimating students' abilities based on media portrayals of ability).[13] While some students deviate from my guidelines, I typically ask pairs or trios of students to create a three-panel drawing consisting of two panels that depict the moment and one panel that shows how they might disrupt the imbalance of power (for specific suggestions, see the sidebar "Scenario Comics").

Working in small groups, students jump into the conversation with a different kind of energy than when we are simply discussing a text. Challenged to illustrate their ideas, their discussions move quickly from the conceptual ideas of power and privilege to the real-life examples they must turn into imagery. Doing so forces them to make choices, such as what color to shade a character's skin or how to draw different gender characteristics. Suddenly, the theoretical ideas become more realistic as they step into the scenes they are creating. To turn memories or imagined scenarios into actual images is to give them a new kind of life—one that forces students to question the shape of identity both on the page and in reality.

Once they have created their comics, we gather to discuss. One group has illustrated a job interview in which the lead character, a black woman with her hair styled in an Afro, is asked if she is willing to change her hairstyle once she is in the classroom. Another group portrays the moment when a colleague complains that she "wishes that the boys would just dress like boys." In another comic, students have drawn a parent-teacher conference where the teacher tells a parent not to worry, "even disabled students can make art." As we discuss each comic, we refer to the images to help us ask questions about the power dynamics at play in each scene. Like actors stepping onto a stage, we sometimes act out the final panel, wondering what we might do differently to prevent the scenario from occurring or recurring. At other times, I will ask the students to use a red or blue pencil, like fictional editors, to notate where power and identity interact. With a physical image in front of them, students can question what they see. And, just as McCloud notes, they can begin to imagine themselves in the image, allowing them to turn inward and wonder what they might do when power and identity collide in their own teaching.

Scenario Comics

Identify a powerful moment to depict: Choose moments that resonate with students' contexts, ideally taken from what they have witnessed or experienced themselves. Focus on moments that sparked discomfort and that highlight the challenging dynamics of power between students, teachers, administrators, families, and communities. Often these moments are also shaped by our assumptions related to race, class, gender, nationality, ability, and so on. You can find examples by asking students to submit anonymous examples, researching local news reports, or drawing from educational scholarship.

Ask critical questions: Provide a set of questions to help learners analyze the scenario as they create their comics. Questions can start with the observational and move to the more critical: What do you see happening here? What is your immediate emotional reaction? Who holds power in this scenario? What forms of power does each character hold? What assumptions might each character be making about the others? Whose perspective is missing? What social and/or political factors (i.e., race, economic wealth, academic status, etc.) are at play in this scenario?

Use the tools of comic art: Consider how comics can help us tell stories through the use of symbolic imagery, framing and cropping, perspective and pacing, and narrative. Encourage students to ask critical questions to identify the key aspects of the story to depict. For example, have them consider when power is most apparent and then focus their imagery on that moment, perhaps zooming in to a particular detail or zooming out to show a wider perspective. Discuss how artists use symbols and simplified images to highlight the various kinds of power each character carries.

Develop strategies to reduce harm: Instruct students to use the final panel of their comic strip to reimagine a different outcome. Ask students to develop both immediate, short-term responses to the scenario and long-term strategies that could dismantle the power imbalances, cultural assumptions, and harm that exists in the original scenario. In depicting those, encourage students to wonder—and draw—what alternative outcomes might be possible.

Practical Considerations for Implementation

Select relevant scenarios: A comic is only as good as the story it tells. To ensure that participants have rich content to work with, carefully consider the scenarios to illustrate. Unfortunately, examples of cross-identity conflict abound. In addition to sourcing stories from local news reports, educators might use the opportunity to interview each other or other community members about their experiences with identity. Such discussions can yield anecdotes about identity that may be deeply rooted in local contexts. When compiling possible scenarios for comics, educators might provide a list of examples to choose from. Alternatively, participants could mine their own reflections on how their identities have played a role in their teaching and learning; certainly, these personal stories would provide meaningful moments for illustration.

Ask questions: Questions beget questions. To help students practice a critical analysis of the scenarios they choose to draw, I provide a series of reflection questions. These questions range from basic observational questions (What were the first images that came into your head? What race, class, gender, age, culture, sexual orientation, and so on were the characters? How do you know?) to questions that seek to air possible biases (How might these reactions affect your interpretation of the situation?). In discussions of the resulting comics, I pose questions to prompt expansive thinking about how we each experience identity. The goal here is to move questions beyond a surface-level analysis to uncover a more nuanced view of how power shapes our relationships. Without the space to question how social messages shape how we relate to each other, we cannot wonder whether and how our relationships might be different. For example, when I ask, "What are some possible reasons for the characters' behaviors or comments?" I find that students are challenged to step into the comic strip itself to imagine possible explanations for the scenario. Finally, as we debrief the process, we must take time to answer questions about how they might respond to a similar scenario, both in the moment and for the long term. When I ask, "What could you do to check your initial reactions or assumptions?" students wonder about possible strategies they could enact in their daily lives.

Encourage critical analysis: When creating artwork about moments when our identity has mattered to us or to someone else, we might want to hide our emotional reactions. Silence makes for an easy cover. Often, when creating these comics, I overhear some students quietly admit to knowing exactly what the characters in the scenario have experienced. Perhaps they have been the one who was ridiculed by a classmate, or the one who stood by silently while a colleague told a sexist joke. Our emotional reactions are real. Unfortunately, we are often taught to ignore those reactions when it comes to our social and cultural identities. There are prescribed ways to react; typically those reactions are mediated by the codes of dominant identity groups (i.e., white, male, heterosexual, Christian, American). This is especially the case in education, where we are often taught that the work of teaching and learning is a neutral process of learning facts to build knowledge. Nothing could be further from the truth, especially when we teach and learn about identity.

As Beverly Tatum reminds us in her book, *Why Are All the Black Kids Sitting Together in the Cafeteria*, our silence around talking about identity "alienates us not only from others but also from ourselves and our own experiences."[14] To avoid the tendency to keep quiet, participants must use the opportunity to analyze identity scenarios in order to lean into the discomfort of learning how identity shapes our experiences. While the comics can provide a cushion of sorts for this learning, facilitators must remind participants of the terms of engagement and to cultivate a sense of trust among the group. To soften entry into a discussion, they might introduce examples of other comics (for example, Marjane Satrapi's *Persepolis* or Gene Luen Yang's *American Born Chinese*) as introductory materials before shifting to more personal scenarios. Additionally, facilitators can model caring curiosity by asking open-ended questions to prompt wondering about the artworks at hand. In doing so, they can encourage participants to focus on the artwork rather than their own fear of sharing.

Animating theory, visualizing silence: Often when teaching and learning about identity (and especially the connections between identity and power), educators will either avoid theory altogether or fail to connect it meaningfully to reality. The benefit of creating comics is that the art form itself merges text and image in a narrative format. The medium itself can easily accommodate conceptual ideas. In using comics to dissect academic texts, participants can practice making theoretical ideas real; they can give actual legs to abstract ideas. Educators can use theory as a tool to analyze each comic, pointing to illustrated examples of a concept as it plays out in the lived or imagined experiences within the comics.

ACTIVITY 2

While wondering about one's own identity can be challenging, to intentionally wonder about someone else while making a work of art can feel particularly daunting.

Conversation Portraits

The anxiety in the room is palpable when I describe the two-part assignment of attending a public event and creating a "conversation portrait." The students tentatively ask, "Wait, you mean we have to go someplace where we will be the outsider? And we have to then talk to someone?" In a room filled with educators—some who have already been working with young people in various capacities for many years—I'm always surprised by the fear that this assignment elicits. Conversations are hardly a mysterious format. We are accustomed to talking with strangers in encounters at the grocery store or when ordering a coffee and in higher-stakes situations such as job interviews or even blind dates. This particular group of New Yorkers definitely interacts with hundreds of strangers each day as we navigate the city. Yet, the challenge to talk to someone outside our typical social circles is nerve-racking for many. Their apprehension is testament to the strength of the socially constructed walls that prevent us from knowing each other, and a reminder of how important it is to breach those walls.

The conversation portrait consists of several interrelated elements. First, students must attend a public event in the community they are getting to know. Whether a festival, special program, community meeting, civic meeting, religious service, or informal gathering, these public events should give students a chance to meet people in a social atmosphere. To further nudge them outside their comfort zones, the conversation activity requires students to talk to someone—even briefly—in an effort to learn about their life experiences. Framed as a conversation, these are really simply casual chats. In class, I often encourage students to just try to talk with someone, to get to know something about them, and to find some kind of connection. (In the sidebar "Conversation Portraits," I note some of the general parameters and prompts I design for this activity.)

Once students have had a conversation with someone, they must create a portrait of their experience. Taken broadly, a portrait is a representation of someone. Artists, however, have been known to play with the definition of a portrait. They have created portraits out of every imaginable material. Sometimes the portraits contain a recognizable image of a human; at other times, they only hint at a human presence. Often they are as much self-portrait as other-portrait, turning the focus on the creator as well as the subject. The portraits created for this assignment have been no different. Some students have painted realistic representations of the person they met. Others have filmed abstract videos that allude to a moment in the conversation. One student printed a repeating phrase on an unfurling roll of receipt paper. Another created a collaged book that folded onto itself like an accordion. Once there was a coffee mug. There have been mobiles, wearable art, sculptures, poems, and, of course, photographs.

In class, we spend time looking closely at each portrait, as students reflect on their experiences. Typically, a pattern emerges in their reflections about their experiences talking with people outside their social circles: "I was scared and nervous." "I almost didn't go." "I stood outside in the cold for ten minutes giving myself a pep talk before I could walk in the door." "I was so worried that people would be mean to me, that I'd make a mistake and offend someone, that I would not do or say the right thing." "I was sweating through my shirt." "The event had already begun, so I snuck in the back and tried to be as inconspicuous as possible." "After several minutes, I decided to try to say hello to someone . . . or actually, someone approached me to welcome me and introduce themselves." "They were kind!" "I told them I was there for a class assignment to get to know people better." "They were intrigued." "They asked about me!" "They told me to come in and make myself at home." "I was so surprised at how warm and welcoming they were." "This was not what I expected at all." "I had been taught this community would not want me around, and well, maybe that's not the case." "I had been taught this community was cold or insular or exclusive or . . . and maybe my expectations were wrong." "It wasn't as hard as I thought." And, it almost always ends with, "I think I could and would do it again."

Conversation Portraits

Find a public event: Although the internet can offer an easy way to find many local public events, often the best route is to read local newspapers, stop by posting boards in cafés or grocery stores, or consult with local community, religious, or government centers. Students should identify events that are open to the public; if it is unclear, they should contact organizers to ensure that outsiders are welcome. Ideally, students attend the public event alone (bringing along a friend often limits potential interactions with new people).

Introduce yourself: At the event itself—or in any interaction with a community member—students should introduce themselves and explain their interest in learning more. Conversations typically start small, with shared comments; possible topics can include the weather, local news, shared food, or recent movie or sports references. Often it is easy to just start by asking someone, "How was your day?" or "What are your weekend plans?" If students feel anxious, they can practice small talk and simple introductions with a friend before venturing out.

Ask questions, listen intently, share ideas: As in any good conversation, students should aim to ask genuine questions, to listen with honest care, and to share their own views. Depending on the setting, initial questions can center on the activities of the public event (i.e., "Have you been here before?" "What drew you to come?" "What do you think of the food, music, speaker, topic, etc.?"). Students should pay attention to social cues and listen for what people are both saying and not saying. If it feels appropriate, students may ask deeper questions such as, "Have you noticed any changes within this community in recent years?" or more personal questions such as, "How does your connection to this community play a role in your life?" Students should also be prepared to answer any question they ask, leaning toward their own vulnerability in sharing ideas with a new person.

Reflect on the experience: Immediately after the conversation, students should take stock of their own emotional and mental reactions: What was surprising? Were there moments that felt awkward? How did the actual experience compare with their expectations? As students ask these questions, they can record their responses and work to analyze their own reactions by asking themselves why these thoughts and emotions emerged.

Capture reactions in a portrait: After reflecting on the conversation experience, students should look for patterns or telling moments that highlight how the experience of the conversation affected them. Rather than creating a portrait of the appearance of the person they talked with, they should create a portrait of what was shared between them. In this way, they might focus on their own emotional reactions or moments of learning. Students should use art materials that contribute to the story they want to tell about their conversation experience.

Practical Considerations for Implementation

Honest intentions and genuine curiosity: Writing about the importance of getting to know students as individuals, Joshua Aronson reminds us that "true curiosity is not a tactic: it is a mindset that cannot be faked."[15] When starting a conversation or interview with someone, one must come with genuine compassion and honest intentions. I often encourage students to share something about why they are interested in getting to know more about a specific community. This can serve to both initiate a conversation and establish a sense of trust. To help students nurture their own honest curiosity, I encourage them to start their interview conversation with real questions they have about the community they are getting to know. Questions such as these can prompt open-ended and respectful discussions: How are they connected to this community? How do they describe its history? How do they feel this community is perceived? How would they like it to be perceived? As students adjust these questions based on their own interests, they can develop an approach to talking to people that feels true to who each of them is.

Talk with *people*: A common pitfall when initiating a conversation outside one's typical social spheres is to maintain an outsider mentality. When students envision themselves as journalists trying to interview someone on their opinions about a community, they ensure that distance will remain between themselves and the interviewee. Journalism strives for this kind of objective reporting, whereby the person asking the questions and taking notes does not cross lanes to come too close to the person answering the questions. Nothing could be more damaging to the potential to find connections and build relationships across communities. Not only does this stance model that of the colonial anthropologist studying groups of people from afar, but it also fails to allow any room for self-reflection. While students may learn some information, they will do little to reveal anything about their own reactions and therefore will not leave any opportunity for reciprocal conversation, critical wondering, or shared empathy.

To help students avoid this very common challenge, we spend time discussing how to approach people. I often find myself coaching students in small talk. Yet, the ability to forge an initial connection based on genuine care and the hope for real reciprocity is imperative here. Without this, we easily adhere to the socially constructed lines that separate us from each other. To cross those lines, we must be brave in our willingness to engage in conversations that afford chances for mutual growth. Students should remind themselves of the terms of engagement as they seek humility and compassion in their interactions with other people.

Focus on the experience, not just the person: To help students cultivate a stance toward wondering, the conversation portrait exercise asks students to create a portrait of the *experience* of the interview, not just the person they met. The aim here is to shift the emphasis away from meeting a person just to capture their likeness in a work of art to meeting a person to find some reciprocal connection. Moving the focus to the experience of the conversation prompts students to also consider what the conversation meant for them. To support this, I typically provide questions that students can ask themselves throughout the interview and as they create their final portraits: What stands out to you about the experience? What do you notice about your own reactions? How do people interact with you or with each other? How did you feel? What surprised you? In reflecting on these questions, students expand their view of a conventional portrait to include their own perspectives and reactions.

Include yourself in the portrait: When students start to work on their portraits, they can find it hard to break out of the conventional views of what a portrait should be: an image of another person. However, just as every academic paper carries the biases of its writer, every portrait also bears the fingerprints of its creator. And those fingerprints tell equally important stories about who we are in relation to each other. When we neglect to acknowledge ourselves in the portraits we create, we erase the connections between ourselves and the people we meet. We add to the view that they are separate from us; their otherness is maintained. As students turn their attention to transforming their experiences into a visual record, I prod them to think critically about their own role in the conversation. I often repeatedly ask them to revisit the critical questions they asked themselves as they sought to expand the focus of the interview to include their own questions and reactions. What did they notice about their own thoughts during the conversation? What surprises stuck with them? When did they find themselves nodding in agreement? What connections emerged? What do their reactions tell them about how they have been taught to see themselves and other people? Questions such as these can help students think about how they might portray themselves within the final portrait. Sometimes this may be as simple as including a representation of themselves in the final portrait—an allusion to their favorite color or the tea they were drinking during the conversation. At other times, they might directly focus on how the portrait is shaped by their own eyes by asking viewers to look through a portal to see the image. These strategies draw our attention toward the ways in which our existence is intimately linked to and shaped by those around us.

Share the portrait: While students may not always follow this suggestion, I encourage everyone to share the final visual portrait with the person they talked to. Although many students are nervous about doing so, this small action honors the time and energy that was granted to the student. Having someone create a work of art about a moment you shared is a rare gift; few people would turn down the chance to see the final result. Furthermore, by sharing the portrait, students include the person they met in the entire activity—nothing is hidden. While some may feel vulnerable showing their artwork, they should remember that they asked for vulnerability from the person they met; to reciprocate is to respect that original offering.

Learning to Wonder: Turning Inward

When students learn to wonder about who they are and the factors that influence how they relate to other people, they unlock the rigidity of their own thinking—a move that allows for new interpretations. Through using art to critically analyze the social and power dynamics that affect relationships between people, their understanding of the human dimensions of power and privilege deepen. Whereas we often use theoretical texts to help students learn about social inequity, the arts provide spaces for students to visually and viscerally step into the shoes of another person and to imagine how the world looks from another perspective.

Imagining ourselves in the story: One of the most useful features of many forms of art is that they encourage us to wonder what it is like to see the world through someone else's perspective. This can happen when we look at a work of art, as described in chapter 2, but also when we create an image ourselves. The act of rendering our thoughts into a physical artwork prods us to question the most effective way to tell a story. As we do, we end up thinking about the story from different angles. This kind of multifaceted reflection helps us nurture a more expansive understanding of the story we aim to tell. Often, it also prompts us to consider what it might be like to be each character within the story.

When we imagine ourselves as other characters within a story, we see ourselves from the outside. This out-of-body like experience can push students to consider their own assumptions. As Jose-Manuel, a former student, talked about his experience making art in my course, he noted how the process fostered self-reflection about his own perspectives: "It made me ask myself: How do others perceive me? Also, asking myself: What biases are in place that make me treat that person in this particular way? How can I break some of those assumptions? . . . To me it's been more a discovery than anything." For Jose-Manuel and many other students, drawing a story provides an opportunity to question what it might feel like to be a part of that story and to wonder just how we might respond.

Learning to critically analyze relationships: As students think about the scenario they are creating, they often find themselves wondering why something happens. This important question can launch critical analyses of the multiple ways we each experience the world. Describing her own teaching, Jasmin pointed out that "you have to constantly ask, 'Why?' Like that's like the whole reason for like galleries and museums and stuff. People are . . . walking around and they might not say 'why?' out loud, but every now and then a 'why?' thought might pop in their head about a piece of artwork like, 'I wonder why he chose to do this.'" This inquiry triggers additional questions. She continued, "Like, even if it's something like at a basic level like, 'I wonder why he chose to paint the ocean?' Like, 'what does the ocean mean to this particular person?'" Then we compare those questions to our own reactions: "Ocean to me might mean the ocean my ancestors had to pass over. Whereas the ocean to someone else may mean 'how they go on yachts with their dad' and I have no clue about stuff like that. But then, [I start to think] 'How does it feel to be on a private yacht with your dad? Why does your dad have so much money? Oh! Because his granddad owned a few slaves? That's pretty crazy because those might have been the slaves that were on that ship that I was just thinking about sailing over that same ocean.' And then that's the part where it probably starts to get uncomfortable for people." That's the part when the discomfort can lead to learning.

Humanizing theory: Trying to help students analyze complex ideas about identity—particularly how power and privilege (or the lack of it) shape who we are in relation to each other—can be daunting. Words can sometimes only get us so far in the conversation. Sometimes we need another vantage point to animate the theories, research, and reporting. And when we do, it can have a profound effect on how students question and process their learning. Jane recalls the moment when questions about a work of art became suddenly personal: "We were all listing our different things [identities] and . . . we eventually get to this point where it's 'identity's constructed.' And I'm like 'wow!' because the whole time, the moment you asked that question is was like split seconds later . . . there was this other side . . . What is that? What is that? It was like this swirling tunnel that was sort of this awakening that I hadn't ever considered my identity and then I hadn't considered what had been constructed inside of me." In a matter of a few moments, Jane's understanding of the concept of a socially constructed identity shifted as she wondered about a work of art. And the questions kept coming: "[I started thinking about] where I was coming from, and what that meant? . . . I have been told so many times my whole life and do I even believe that that's my identity? And I was like 'actually I don't think I do.' . . . Like I've been told what you wear doesn't matter, your race doesn't matter, all these things don't matter which, in reality, it does matter. You *do* have to talk about those things . . . That was hard, that was an awakening." Sometimes, in wondering about an artwork, the challenging conceptual ideas of identity, for example, how it is socially constructed, can come suddenly and vividly to life.

Learning to Wonder: Leaning Outward

When challenged to physically step outside their typical social circles to meet and interact with new people, students have the chance to learn how other people experience the world. As they listen to people and reflect on their conversations with others, they practice wondering about the connections that they might not have previously noticed, the porousness of the walls between people, and the potential relationships they can build with people different from them.

Gaining insight about themselves: Sometimes, asking questions is scary, and it can be even more unnerving when we are talking to people we don't know well. Paired with a portrait assignment, this arts-based conversation challenge gives students a framework to talk with people. In conversations, the questions go both ways. While they might initiate the discussion, they inevitably end up answering questions themselves. Again, the context sets students up to reflect on who they are in relation to someone else. When she interviewed her next-door neighbor, an older man to whom she had only ever nodded a passing greeting, Jackie, a former student, came to learn more about herself than about her neighbor: "I think it definitely made me think more about my identity. Talking to my neighbor and where my neighbor was coming from made me have to reveal myself, like where I'm coming from and where my family is from. Because in order to ask my neighbor to reveal himself, I had to do the same, otherwise there wasn't going to be any trust and connection there. Yeah, it wasn't just a one-way interview." As Jackie points out, good conversation requires a kind of mutual respect. And a good conversation can spark curiosity: "It made me think about what I was comfortable doing in my community and what was possible for me, or what was I interested in doing. And it also made me think about difference in like the places I go and who I am in those places, and what I offer, and the people I interact with." As Jackie experienced, a good conversation can stick with us, leave us wondering and wanting more.

Nurturing empathy: In advising them to break through socially constructed ways of interacting across difference, I ask students to take a risk. In many ways, these risks are akin to those that our own students experience as they step foot into our classrooms—trying to quickly figure out who we are as their teachers, what we value, how we communicate, why we do what we do. And we forget that our students may regularly experience this same trepidation as they learn to navigate the world. As educators in positions of relative power to our students, we forget that we are asking them to step out of their comfort zones and to trust the community we are trying to create in our classrooms. A large part of our work is to connect quickly with our students—no matter how different from us they might be.

The chance to talk with someone, to really listen carefully and to ask thoughtful questions of each other with intentionality, forces us to consider another perspective. Jasmin points out that even just a "general getting to know somebody" can shift how we understand them: "Because sometimes just letting someone know exactly what's going on with you, outside of whatever place you're in, might give them a hint as to why you're different than them." Learning a little more about someone can open giant possibilities for empathy. But it isn't easy. Jasmin continues, "The empathy part is hard though. You kind of have to make somebody live through that [your] experience as best as you can in order for them to relate with you fully. And that takes a long time, sometimes. Sometimes it happens fast, but most of the time it takes a very long time." Empathy takes time and requires that we learn to question and wonder outside of ourselves. Educator-scholar Lisa Delpit writes, "To put our beliefs on hold" in order to examine them, "is to cease to exist as ourselves for a moment—and that is not easy. It is painful as well, because it means turning yourself inside out, giving up your own sense of who you are, and being willing to see yourself in the unflattering light of another's angry gaze. It is not easy, but it is the only way to learn what it might feel like to be someone else and the only way to start the dialogue."[16]

Slowing down: When creating portraits of the people they chatted with, students spend time reflecting on their experiences. Slowing down to compose a work of art about the moments of boundary crossing gives them the opportunity to think slowly and reflect deeply about their experience. Often as we discuss their final portraits, they mention how much they had to work to capture the spirit of the conversation, or the awkwardness of the moment, or the unexpected connection they experienced. Artwork doesn't come quickly, and the time and reflection it requires gives students a chance to replay their interactions with the person they talked to. In turning the words over and looking at them from different vantage points, students ask themselves questions about the conversation. Did I understand that right? Did I miss something? Why was it so different than my expectations? Rarely do I even need to state these questions out loud. Students describe being able to reconsider interactions that they had thought were unsettling in the moment but now, in retrospect, are actually able to empathize with the person and see the conversation through their eyes. They realize that perhaps people are more complex than they seem and that the lines that divide us are much less opaque. The task of creating a portrait of their experience stirs a sense of wondering about both the person they encounter and their own reactions. As they craft their visual portraits, their sense of empathy deepens.[17]

Establishing relationships: As students expand their capacity to empathize with those who they previously thought were distant strangers, they see more connections than barriers. Confronting their own fears about other people and the social cues they've been taught, they see those fears as unfounded. Once the fear is replaced with compassion, there is room to establish a relationship. Mateo, a former student, described his shifting understanding when he talked to someone he met at a religious gathering:

> I went to a couple of sessions of—what was it called—"Progressive Muslims of New York," or something like that. They had a meet-up group and more than anything it was just the eye-opening conversations we had about beliefs and faiths and worldviews. That was very useful for me because, you know, I never had really close Muslim friends before, and establishing a relationship with that guy that I met, and having two different worldviews, sit and have coffee and talk about, "How do you see the world?" That was very enriching to me.

After their initial conversations, several of the students maintained contact with the people they met. Occasionally, the conversations start longer relationships. This is especially the case for students who interview neighbors, colleagues, or immediate community members. Jackie described: "It was neat to have a conversation together [with my neighbors] and have a deeper relationship with them; they're people I see every day." Not that it is always this easy. Sometimes the conversations have started on rocky ground, as when the building superintendent in Juliette's apartment snapped at her for coming to say hello only when she needed something. Yet, even that moment marked a shift in their relationship; Juliette apologized and took the time to ask the superintendent more about her life. Another student was thrilled when her initial conversation with a neighbor turned into multiple conversations. The beginning of a relationship seemed to unfold easily until the moment her neighbor requested sponsorship for an immigrating cousin; suddenly, the student and her neighbor were navigating new dimensions of power related to their different citizenship status. Although the student described the conversations as challenging, both she and her neighbor came to a mutual understanding of how to continue to build a relationship across their very different life experiences and social identities. While not every conversation leads to a newfound relationship, we can be confident that no relationship magically appears without an initial connection.

During our final debrief for the conversation portraits, Kirstin, a soft-spoken and self-pronounced introvert, pipes up. "I was terrified to do this assignment," she begins. "I was sure that people would be mean to me or ignore me entirely." I watch as several other students nod their heads emphatically. She is not alone. "But then I started talking to this older woman. And she was so kind to me. We ended up having tea together in her little café. She told me all about the neighborhood. I eventually gave her the little watercolor I made of us sharing our tea. Now, when I pass by, I stop and say hi." The interaction Kirstin had could have lasted more than an hour—plus the additional hours to create the portrait. Either way, it's not a lot of time. Yet, in this sliver of a moment—sharing tea and making a watercolor—Kirstin has also created a tiny connection with someone who was once a stranger. "It was totally scary," she continues, "but I think I'd try it again."

CHAPTER 4

Researching Stance

Dominator culture has tried to keep us all afraid, to make us choose safety instead of risk, sameness instead of diversity. Moving through that fear, finding out what connects us, revelling in our differences; this is the process that brings us closer, that gives us a world of shared values, of meaningful community.[1]

—bell hooks

MORE THAN ONLY DREAM CATCHERS

When I ask students to write down everything that comes to mind when I say the phrase, "Native American art," they immediately jump to the task. Pencils race and the lists stretch down the pages of their notebooks. When we start to share those lists on the board, the results form the same image every time: "feathers," "moccasins," "beads," "pottery," "animal hides," "nature," "spirituality," "tipis," "totem poles," "powwows," "headdresses," and always, "dream catchers." We stand back and look at the list; the stereotypes are glaring.[2] Someone points out that all they have ever learned about Native American people comes from movies and a single chapter in their American history textbooks. Rarely can anyone name any of the tribes local to the New York region (though they can sometimes name the casinos). On the class computer, I type the words "Native American art lesson plan" into Google, and pages worth of sites pop up. We click on one of the first ones; a major American art supply company posts lesson plans for educators to download for immediate use in their classrooms. Together, we dissect the lesson description; the problems are rampant: "Native American Indians are famous for their beautiful turquoise and silver jewelry and belts. The Indians, who were very close to the earth and spiritual people, believed that certain animals, birds, etc. possessed special powers."[3] Which Native Americans does this refer to, we wonder. Were they really *all* spiritual? What does it mean to be "close to the earth"? And where were the Native American people on the East Coast finding turquoise? We compare the lesson plan to our list and see too many parallels. The stereotypes are winning. One student relates a story about a teacher she overheard telling her fourth-grade class that Native Americans no longer exist. Another student chimes in to say that's what she learned in school too. Research on how poorly Native American history and contemporary life are taught across the country confirms their anecdotes.[4] Forget stereotypes; for too many people, outright lies shape our views of Native American people. Unfortunately, this same kind of surface-skimming stereotypical information also forms our assumptions about many social and cultural communities.

As we return to our own lists, we talk about what it means to teach about a community that is not your own. Do we have the right? What can we do to avoid the kind of superficial and, frankly, wrong information we see on our own lists? In small groups, students set out to answer these questions. Some of the groups turn to their own identities to consider how they might create a lesson about their cultural heritage. Other groups consider the tools of research that artists often employ as they generate ideas for new creative projects. Each cluster of students wrestles with how to balance their own identity perspectives—their positionality—with the challenge of teaching about another person's perspectives, traditions, and life experiences. By the end of the session, each group shares their criteria for further collective critique. The criteria are almost always the same: be specific about the time periods, locations, and names of communities; discuss connections across time, location, and cultural communities; work with primary sources (people, documents, materials); confirm and critique the accuracy of information from multiple sources; be transparent about our own knowledge (especially when it's limited); and critically examine the ethical dimensions of our teaching. While looking at this list together, without fail someone will always declare: "This list is so helpful, but it sure sounds a lot more complicated than what I had thought I'd do." A few people laugh. And then we all agree that that is probably a good sign.

෴   ෴   ෴

At its most fundamental level, "[r]esearch," as the novelist and folklorist Zora Neale Hurston famously explained, "is formalized curiosity."[5] In other words, it is to systematically search for understanding with intention. Through research, we identify patterns, points of convergence and divergence, and connections. More so than simply gathering information about a topic, research requires us to hold what we learn up to the light, to look at it with squinting eyes to see what else we can learn from what we have found. Research is about mapping the context of an idea or topic, of seeing the web of factors and relationships that link together. As we research and contextualize, our awareness of the complexity and nuance of an idea deepens. For educators, our capacity to bring a critical curiosity to how we think about our identity and the identities of those around us can make the difference between perpetuating dangerous stereotypes and promoting a multifaceted understanding of who we are in relation to each other.

In educational settings across the United States, educators regularly design lesson plans that aim to teach about the cultural traditions and identities of people who are somehow different than they are. Many schools require teachers to teach special units related to public holidays or culturally related theme months. Because so many of us have been taught a primarily Eurocentric, heteronormative, Judeo-Christian, patriarchal, and white-washed account of our nation's cultural history, rarely do educators have the depth of knowledge about cultural and social identities outside what we've been taught ourselves. The lists that students make in class of their first associations with Native American art would vary in content, but not in depth for many other identity groups, such as women, queer, disabled, Arab American, and so on. So when educators quickly create lessons related to the stories of Thanksgiving, Chinese New Year, Black History Month, Women's History Month, or Indigenous People's Day (or, as it's known in some places, Columbus Day), it is no surprise that the lessons often rely on inaccurate or stereotypical understandings of identity.

Although educators do not swear to any kind of Hippocratic Oath like our colleagues in the medical field, we still need to seek to do no harm as we teach students how to make sense of the world. This means moving beyond surface understandings of identity to critically analyze the ways in which our identities are nuanced, complex, and shifting. To do this, we have to be serious about researching the contexts and factors that influence our views of ourselves and each other. This means studying the histories—both the dominant and the counternarratives—of the communities we teach in, with, and about. We must scour as many resources as possible—primary sources, films, artwork, fiction, poetry, music, posters, oral histories—to learn from multiple perspectives. We must be alert to possible connections. And as we do this, we must examine the information we gather with critical eyes. The simple accumulation of information does not inoculate us from perpetuating inaccurate or stereotypical ideas about communities. Without an acknowledgment of the impact of systemic power and privilege on our multiple identities, any attempt at building relationships across difference runs the risk of remaining at the surface or, worse, perpetuating negative biases and assumptions.

Writing about research, scholar Eve Tuck proposes a framework that is "concerned with understanding complexity, contradiction, and the self-determination of lived lives."[6] When Tuck advocates for a more nuanced approach to research, she reminds us of what she seeks to upend: the legacy of research that was (is) done to or on groups of people, often without their consent or against their will. Although she writes primarily for academic researchers, her words ring true for any of us who seek to develop a more robust understanding of a group of people—especially one that we have been trained to see as "other"—when she encourages researchers to reconsider how they might do work *with* not *about* or *on* communities.[7] With this in mind, educators need also remember to research identity-focused lessons with a critical compassion that can help them delve below surface views of identity *with* people.

WHAT THE ARTS TEACH US ABOUT RESEARCHING

Artists, it is often said, traffic in stories. They create narratives that transport us to new worlds or back in time to experience other eras, regions, or moments. They spin tales that tell us who we are, should be, were, or might have been. To study and to make these stories is to engage with ideas about who we are and what that means. To create a work of art is to choose a specific story to share—perhaps to reveal or highlight a particular truth in the world. Likewise, to encounter a work of art is to enter that story, to gain insight into that particular perspective. Stories, like research, are tools for both gathering information and for sharing it. This is why it is no surprise that Zora Neale Hurston drew simultaneously from her training as a folklorist studying African American folklore and her formidable storytelling skills to write books (both fiction and nonfiction) that deepened and stretched readers' understanding of African American identities. Like most artists, she knew that in collecting, telling, and retelling stories, we learn about who we are.

Although thinking about research as storytelling may feel like a reach for some who have been taught to view research as something that takes place in a sanitized lab with certified scientists dressed in white lab coats, research is a common practice among artists, even those who don't carry clipboards. Artists use research to unearth hidden connections, to track down untold stories, to draw attention to overlooked details in our world. In doing so, they seek to gain a greater understanding of the context of a topic or idea and then, though their art, to make the web of relationships visible. For some artists, this may mean spending time in a space, drawing sketches, observing details, and taking preparatory photographs in order to really know a location before painting a landscape or creating a mural. For other artists, research might entail hours in libraries, archives, or family attics as they piece together remnants of history to compile a more nuanced story. Some artists conduct research by simply talking to people, taking notes or recording their words, while others turn inward, researching their own reactions through diaries, free associations, and self-reflection. Regardless of the format, as artist Mark Addison Smith notes, research enables artists "to break down a topic in order to build it back up into a more focused, layered outcome."[8] For artists, research—or Hurston's "formalized curiosity"—is the means by which they gather information in order to share it.

If we are to think about works of art as records of the information that the artist has collected, analyzed, and translated into visual (or auditory, sensory) form, then we can see art as portals to help us understand different and more deeply layered perspectives about identity. Photographer Sarah Sense, who describes her family heritage as both Choctaw and Chitimacha, was interested in exploring Hollywood-inspired imagery of Native Americans. As she researched the stories in her own family traditions, she learned about importance of basket weaving: "After researching the history of Chitimacha basket weaving, I was inspired to continue the tradition of my ancestors."[9] Sense knew that she would need permission from the elders in her community in order to incorporate traditional basket-weaving patterns into her work: "In 2004, the chairman of the Chitimacha Tribe of Louisiana gave me permission to use nontraditional material in weaving our basket patterns, and since then I have incorporated photographic images into my work."[10] Slicing her photographs into strips, Sense weaves imagery together to create photographic tapestries: "I began by weaving reservation landscapes. The images evolved as I incorporated Hollywood posters, family photo archives, and my personas of 'The Cowgirl' and 'The Indian Princess.'"[11] Sense's artwork brings together in-depth research into her own cultural identity as well as how that identity is portrayed by others—a move that helps her and her viewers develop a more nuanced view than what we are typically taught about the all-encompassing "Native American identity."

As artists conduct research, their findings reveal connections that are often ignored in dominant views of identity. Taking inspiration from their findings, they can create works of art that disrupt our conventional ideas about identity. Brian Jungen, an artist from Canada and the Dunne-za First Nation, was motivated to make artwork that challenged the stereotypical views he heard in what he called his "reverse ethnographic study" of people's thoughts about native people: "I started to do a lot of drawings that were taking advantage of stereotypes that exist of Indian folks." He used these drawings in his work as "a way of kind of reclaiming the term 'Indian.'"[12] In his larger-scale sculptures, Jungen repurposes athletic gear—golf bags, baseball mitts, skiing and hockey bags—to replicate traditional art forms from the indigenous cultures of the Pacific Northwest. He stacks brightly colored Nike and Adidas bags to resemble totem poles, or refashions Air Jordans into the form of a Tlingit mask. His works, based on in-depth research, highlight contemporary connections that complicate conventional flat views of native identity.

The stories that artists such as Sense and Jungen tell through their artwork are both the result of extensive research and opportunities for viewers to develop a more nuanced awareness of the context in which these artworks exist. To create these works, Sense and Jungen dove deeply into the connections between their own cultural backgrounds, contemporary stereotypes, popular culture, history, modern and traditional materials, culturally specific aesthetic patterns and processes, and their own personal life experiences. As they created their work, they crafted stories that wove together these various connections into a more complex narrative—a web of sorts—that can challenge our understandings of how we perceive ourselves and others.

As artist Hương Ngô notes, "Research makes the creative work more difficult, but also more layered, specific, and for me, more rewarding. I think that every artist does research in some way, whether it is visual, material, historical, ethnographic, biographical . . . What is powerful about an artist doing research is that it may fall outside of the typical academic realm, which challenges conventional notions of knowledge production and distribution."[13]

Extending this concept into teaching, Avery, a former student, points out how research enables us to see the textured contexts in which a student's artwork—and by extension their being—exists:

> Art can do this because it is the kind of combination of looking at what someone else has already done and that's participating in the conversation that's already out there—you're looking at a historical context, you're looking at the artists, you're also looking at how you feel about it within the context of your classroom too, and how other people might be looking at it. So you're already starting to get that feeling of how one person might look at it this way but then also getting this great understanding of where this artwork is coming from, what it's reacting to. Then when you're making art, you're turning it and looking at how you feel about you and where you are or in context to something. Making artwork has the ability to make you think in bigger context that hopefully can connect to you. I think art is asking you to think about your self-expression and then tying it to something else—there's this inner and outer connection.

As stories go, works of art are complex. As Avery points out, they demand much of us—both to craft them and to "read" them. They can be sites for exploring multiple perspectives, decoding history, divulging untold narratives, and delving into (so-called) alternative histories. Turning to how we can use art to practice our stance toward a critical curiosity, this chapter looks at two arts-based activities that focus on contextualizing research. The first activity asks students to create a visual timeline of the history of the community they are getting to know. In slowing down to create a work of art, this activity encourages students to rethink their own views and misconceptions about different community histories. The second activity in this chapter moves students into the role of counter-narrator as they alter existing texts to reveal forgotten, misunderstood, or revised versions of history. These activities aim to push our conversations about cross-identity understanding to a deeper level by highlighting how art can help us critically analyze the structural systems that shape our various identities.

ACTIVITY 1

To challenge students to critically analyze the stories they have been taught about different communities, I prompt students to create works of art that document their research on the history of a specific community.

Visual Histories

We are all familiar with timelines—those trusty, date-filled lines in our social studies books. Cousin to the ruler, these recognizable tools help us place events, moments, lives, and histories in some kind of order. In doing so, they help us see the relationships between points in time. Suddenly, seemingly abstract events can be held up as truthful by these connections to each other. A narrative (or multiple narratives) starts to shine through. While leading a group of American students through the Apartheid Museum in Johannesburg, South Africa, recently, I asked students to track a timeline of events in their notebooks to help them make sense of the history they were learning. Halfway through, I asked them to pause and add their own important life markers onto their maps—their birthdays, their family members' birthdays, anniversaries, significant events in their own national and cultural lives. As they did, one student turned to me and said, "Wait a second, this all happened when my grandparents were getting married." I watched her face as she placed a foreign nation's descent into an apartheid state next to her own personal history; a different light flickered on. Suddenly, this history wasn't so distant or abstract.

When I ask students to create a visual timeline of a community's history, there is often an audible sigh of relief. A timeline sounds far simpler and less emotionally risky than actually talking to people in the real world. I tell them that their task is to find as much information as possible about the history of the community they are getting to know, with special attention to its history in New York City (where we are located). I encourage them to consult the internet (using multiple sources to triangulate and fact-check the information), books, newspaper articles, oral histories, fiction, artwork, music, documentaries, and museum archives. Students can use any art form to create their timelines; I urge them to experiment by moving beyond conventional timeline formats to try a three-dimensional or interactive format (see additional suggestions for implementation in the sidebar "Visual Histories").

When sharing their work in class, students unveil wildly different timelines. Created from materials as diverse as mobiles, wire sculpture, and paper scrolls, these visual timelines allow learners to think deeply about the influence of external factors on a community's historical and contemporary context. As we debrief their work, we use the objects in front of us to explore critical questions about the process of creating a record of history. I prompt them to consider if the information was easy or difficult to locate and what sources proved most fruitful. We question how a community's history is typically represented and by whom (and for whom). We wonder about which parts of a community's history are hidden, misrepresented, or more complex than they first appear. And, perhaps more importantly, who benefits or loses from this incomplete telling of a history? Like my student in South Africa, we also use their timelines to examine our own views of history by reflecting on the surprises or discoveries that their research revealed. We question why those surprises matter and what they tell us about how different communities' stories are documented, shared, hidden, highlighted, and critiqued. As our discussions unfold, students' understandings of their timelines deepen. No longer are they simple dots on a line. These timelines, and the stories they carry, morph into objects that deepen our awareness of how we relate to each other's histories. Suddenly, we're all dots on each other's lines.

Visual Histories

Research from multiple sources: The first step is to search for information beyond the internet. Look for oral histories, fiction, poetry, documentary films, artwork, and historical texts from various perspectives. Pay particular attention to primary sources and the documents that emerge from the community members, rather than outsiders.

Look for inconsistencies, surprises, contradictions: Help learners look for discrepancies in the sources they find by directing them to keep a list of inconsistencies, surprises, and contradictions. As they track the incongruities, ask students to consider the following questions: Who is telling the history? Whose perspective is missing? Who benefits (and loses) from this version of history? Who benefits (and loses) by *not* telling parts of a history? What do our surprises tell us about the perspectives of history with which we are most familiar?

Put oneself in the history: As learners piece together their visual histories, encourage them to also include their own life stories. Have them add key moments in their family's history, such as birth dates, anniversaries, important celebrations, dates of emigration, graduations, and so on to their timelines.

Visualize a story about history: To create their visual timeline, learners should consider what story they want to tell about their research. What was notable, surprising, or revealing about their analysis of a community's history? In seeking to illustrate this story of history, they should consider creative strategies that deviate from conventional linear and representational timelines, such as using abstraction, three-dimensionality, or movement.

PRACTICAL CONSIDERATIONS FOR IMPLEMENTATION

Search for many different sources: While we are often taught that history can only be learned in nonfiction history books or archival documents, I regularly encourage students to consider the multiple ways in which historical narratives are documented and shared. For many students, fiction, art, poetry, and films can help them reconsider how history might be told. These arts-based formats help us see how all history is imprinted with the biases and perspectives of the narrator. Furthermore, in seeking out and consulting multiple forms of storytelling, students can practice triangulating their research as they compare one story to another. This kind of comparison can yield conflicting stories—a critical component of historical research.

In her popular TED talk, Chimamanda Ngozi Adichie describes one of the most dangerous pitfalls of researching the stories of a community—the "danger of a single story":

> The single story creates stereotypes, and the problem with stereotypes is not that they are untrue, but that they are incomplete. They make one story become the only story . . . I've always felt that it is impossible to engage properly with a place or a person without engaging with all of the stories of that place and that person. The consequence of the single story is this: It robs people of dignity. It makes our recognition of our equal humanity difficult. It emphasizes how we are different rather than how we are similar.[14]

When teachers base lesson plans on the first story they hear about a group of people or the one narrative they have been taught, they threaten their students' awareness of the complexity of who we are. Single stories are incomplete stories, and, as Eve Tuck reminds us, "incomplete stor[ies are] an act of aggression."[15] These narrow views are fertile ground for limited perceptions of identity—perceptions that breed stereotypes.

Identify and interrogate surprises: As students research the stories within a community, they are likely to come across surprising information. These moments are ripe for introspection. Educators should help students examine why they are surprised, how the introduction of new perspectives might challenge their previous ideas, and how they can make sense of this. As we analyze the visual timelines that students create in class, I push students to locate themselves within the histories they have shared. This can help them identify the points of connection (and divergence) from their own life stories. Often, students are surprised by the many parallels they find when they dig below the surface to deepen their understanding of another community's history. By questioning why those similarities are unexpected, we can see how the socially constructed categories of identity are designed to keep us from an interconnected view of our society's interrelated histories.

Connect history to your own life: As students begin to realize the untold stories, gaps, and missing pieces of their own knowledge about a community's history, they turn their attention inward to consider how their own lives are reflected in and refracted by the histories they study. Through class conversations, we consider how the ways in which some perspectives about history are told and some ignored reveal critical information about who has power in a society. Using our own family stories, we discuss how each member of a family has a different view of shared events; such microcosms give us insight into the ways in which social groups also have different perspectives on historical events. We consider the lasting impact that these stories have on who we think we are and who we think other people are. This move reminds us that history is not a separate entity from our own lives; rather we are deeply connected to the events and ideas that have preceded our current moment in time.

ACTIVITY 2

While visual histories offer opportunities to lean inward to examine our own biases, altered books help us lean outward to reenvision the histories we have been taught.

Altered Books

In art-speak, an altered book is exactly what it sounds like: an artist creatively manipulates the physical form of a book. Altering a book becomes a kind of physical manifestation of rewriting history or offering a counter-narrative. For many students, this can be empowering as they realize they can creatively author their own stories. This might entail adding or entirely removing words, pages, or sections. It might involve the addition of color, lines, shapes, imagery, or collaged materials. Some artists carve directly into the pages of a book, treating it like a block of wood or clay to create a new form. Other artists layer on drawings, prints, or paintings, as if the book itself were a blank canvas. The rules for creating an altered book are few; they simply ask the artists to change a book.

Because so many of us have been taught to treat books with care, this activity can be startling at first. However, after I explain the task, students often relish the permission I have granted to modify a text. As noted in the sidebar "Altered Books," the first step of this activity involves choosing a book. I typically assign this project after the visual timelines and the requirement that students read a work of fiction written by someone from the community they are getting to know. Having thus encountered several texts, I encourage students to choose a book that they feel drawn to alter in some way to offer a more nuanced or complicated story about the community. Over the years, students have selected every type of book, including guidebooks, cookbooks, textbooks, novels, nonfiction, poetry, and children's books. Although this activity does not require that students read an entire book before altering it, I urge them to spend some time with its contents to ensure it is the right choice for their alterations. Once they have grown acquainted with the book, I prompt them to creatively change it.

After completing this activity, nearly every student mentions the initial hurdle of making the first alteration to their chosen book. With such reverence for the written word—especially for those in the field of education—to even decorate a book can feel like damaging it. However, once they begin, students often report a sense of freedom as they seek to tell a new story directly on or within a preexisting story. Often several students perform a kind of "blackout poetry" on the words themselves, redacting large swaths to reveal a kind of found poem from the remaining words. Usually a few students paint or draw directly onto the pages to illustrate conflicting or complementary ideas to the existing text. Some students focus their attention on the cover; a revised title can change the entire meaning of what lies within the book. Others paste in scraps of text and images from other sources—magazines, other books, their own journals—bringing ancient texts into conversation with what they are currently reading.

When we discuss their choices, students often articulate a desire to complicate or challenge the stories they have previously been taught about different communities of people. They scratch out sentences that do not match what they have seen in their research and interactions with people. They create images that illustrate the definitions in a book. They add pages where parts of the published text might be missing. Working within the context of the book form, students realize they can add and subtract ideas to highlight personal connections, critical analyses, and imaginative possibilities. In doing so, they move beyond Ngozi Adichie's "danger of the single story" to unlock the idea that more than one story can be told within the covers of a book.

Altered Books

Pick the right book: The book to be altered should relate to the community history in at least one of several ways. It should tell a story either that directly relates to the community or that can be a stand-in for a parallel or revised version of the community's history (i.e., perhaps a folktale or work of fiction might provide the right allegory for the artist to layer in nonfiction information). It should also be physically appropriate for artistic manipulation (i.e., the paper must be thick enough so ink doesn't bleed through if the artist plans to draw on the pages). The artist should not alter a book that members of a community would consider offensive to damage (i.e., beware of religious texts).

Determine what story should be altered: Through research, identify what alternative or additional perspective has been missing from conventional views of the community's history. Using the list created during the visual timeline, look for surprises, discrepancies, and untold perspectives. Have students consider what they want audiences to learn about the history of the community they are getting to know.

Match the alteration to the text: The creativity of an altered book lies in the many ways in which artists can change the shape, meaning, and format of the book. Encourage learners to find art techniques that match the message they want the audience to learn about the community's history. For example, if they are drawing attention to a lesser-known perspective, perhaps they will want to add additional pages using a larger font or eye-catching colors and foldouts. If they are critiquing existing versions of history, perhaps redacting or cutting out offensive or inaccurate information can convey their critique most effectively.

Practical Considerations for Implementation

Select a book with care and research: When describing this activity, I warn students about choosing the first text they come across. Part of the challenge of creating an altered book is identifying the right book. The books students decide to alter should be connected to the stories they want to learn and share. To find the right book, they must search widely, forcing them to encounter a range of texts, further fueling their research and contextualization of the community they are getting to know. From an aesthetic perspective, students must also find a book that can physically handle manipulation: size, shape, paper quality, length, and format of the text all contribute to the final work of art.

A potential problem of the altered book format is that in some cultures, books are sacred objects that should not be manipulated. To do so would be to desecrate the book and potentially irrevocably damage one's relationship with the very people one might hope to better understand. Because books play such a key role in many communities, it is important to research possible attitudes and beliefs about the printed word as one chooses a book. For example, while Jose-Manuel, a former student, might not have intended harm in selecting the Bible as one of the books he altered, some people in the community of practicing Christians would likely have found his altered book offensive.

Seek contradictions and convergences: As students determine how they would like to creatively alter their chosen book, I urge them to consider the contradictions and convergences they would like to highlight. As is always the case through all of our art-making activities, I pepper them with questions: What about a book aligns with or rejects what you are learning about a specific group of people? What counternarratives or alternative perspectives would you like to make more prominent? How might you use the format of the book to highlight your own reflections as well as those of the people from the community? The point is to constantly encourage expansive and critical questioning of our assumptions and expectations about identity while we create these works of art.

Reimagining history: Part of the task of the altered book is to create an alternative story to the dominant narratives often portrayed in conventional published materials. I encourage students to think both critically and creatively about how we tell our own and each other's stories. To support this, I ask students to reflect on the ways in which history is not always linear nor is it always a move toward progress, as we are often taught in school. Instead, we imagine ways that we might capture the multilayered views of history through altered books, perhaps through writing in missing stories or color-coding various perspectives on the same story. Likewise, students consider how one might create a participatory book with flaps and foldouts to illustrate the ways in which we all are agents in the making of history. Altered books provide a physical manifestation of the ways in which we can learn to think more creatively about the stories about our communities, and to bring those stories into physical reality to share with others.

Learning to Research: Turning Inward

As students practice their ability to research the stories they learn about themselves and other people, they develop a deeper understanding of their own perspectives, blind spots, and biases. They see how power shapes the stories that are told and heard most often. They learn to seek out layers, contradictions, and missing views. And they reflect on the ways in which they have been taught (or not taught) specific versions of history. As they do, their views of the contexts in which we each exist expand and deepen in ways that provide them with a richer critical awareness of the world.

Seeing how power and history intersect: In the afterword to *A People's History of the United States*, Howard Zinn recalls why he wrote about the perspectives so often left out of typical US history texts: "I knew that a historian (or a journalist, or anyone telling a story) was forced to choose, out of an infinite number of facts, what to present, what to omit. And that decision inevitably would reflect, whether consciously or not, the interests of the historian."[16] History, as we are taught it in most classrooms, is nearly always told through the lens of the dominant viewpoint; in the United States, this means through the eyes of white, heterosexual, Christian, male, able-bodied, wealthy citizens. The stories of those outside those identities are often hushed, hidden, ignored, or denied; in other words, they are made invisible by those in power. Remarking on her own sudden awareness, Jennifer, a former student, noted that learning about the history of Coptic Christian immigrants in her community helped her better understand contemporary issues of power: "I realized a lot about discrimination in immigration policy in America. And I had known a little bit of that from high school. I remember I knew about the Chinese Exclusion Act but I didn't realize that it was almost like discrimination was the norm . . . it turns out for most of the time it [US immigration policy] was discriminatory. And so it kind of puts in context things that are happening today with discrimination within immigration."

As students visualize the information they learn about a community's history, they can call forth the many narratives that are often rendered mute. As these stories are given form, students discern new patterns, connections, and narratives that they might not have been able to see through conventional reading of history. Through their creative interpretations of the information they gather, they learn to detect multiple perspectives and views of history. As they do, their awareness of how history influences our identities expands. For example, Jess, a young white woman from the Midwest, had been teaching in a school with predominantly Haitian and Dominican students. Rarely had her school community discussed the national origins of the students, instead focusing on how they were labeled in the United States, as black and Latino students. After observing artwork, reading Junot Díaz's *The Brief Wondrous Life of Oscar Wao*, researching political events of Hispaniola, and creating a visual timeline of the history of the Haitian and Dominican communities in New York, Jess started to understand the histories of her students' home countries in a new way. Jess described how she had realized that some of the tension in her classroom that she had previously attributed to personality conflicts might actually be connected to the history of tension between Haiti and the Dominican Republic, even though her students themselves were not necessarily born in those countries. This realization altered her understanding of her students as she suddenly began to see them within a larger social and historical context.

Realizing that history is not linear: One of the ways in which typical textbook timelines are deceptive is that history is never linear. As professor of indigenous education Linda Tuhiwai Smith warns, a belief in a linear, chronological view of history is in itself a perspective shaped by white, European beliefs about the nature of time.[17] When students are challenged to make visual timelines, they often employ three-dimensional or video-based tools that offer a more expansive view of time. These works of art help them resist simple two-dimensional distortions of history as they expose potential connections between events that are not necessarily focused on time. Whether a sculpture with interwoven wires that highlight crossing moments in time or a handmade garment printed with symbols of a neighborhood's history, these objects enable students to complicate the context in which stories about our past intersect. In doing so, they help us understand ways of seeing and being in the world that we may not have experienced ourselves.

As Olivia, a former student, reflected on her work, there's an "inter-every-thing understanding" that can come from moving outside conventional ways of seeing or reading the world. Works of art can unlock this for us "because you can be transported by a work of art depending on how it touches you. And then learning about the context of it, learning about the intention of it can then help you build an understanding of another time and place, another person, another person's experience that is so outside your own experience." As students learn to think about the narratives of history beyond those told by a one-way line, they can reimagine more expansive and inclusive ways of understanding how we relate to each other and our intersecting histories.

Seeing the people beyond the stereotype: Reminding educators about the damaging effect of single-sided and stereotypical views of people, educator-scholar Leigh Patel writes, "Limiting individuals and even entire populations to a single story dehumanizes because it absolves us of knowing people as three-dimensional and complex humans."[18] When we start to see that people are more than the flat views all too often presented in common media or conventional texts, the stereotypes we've been taught start to fall apart. Suddenly, people and the communities they come from are revealed as more complex and more human. The possibility for greater empathy opens up with each shift in our understanding of the humanity in those around us.

Novice educator Alex reflected on our class discussions about teaching Native American art: "I specifically remember talking about American Indians and the stereotypes, current icons, and false information being provided and taught to students. I believe that this resonated with me because our society has become so fixated on only one perspective of a certain type or group of individuals, and it has been okay in the past to continue this form of derogatory imagery instead of embracing the culture, memories, and traditions that we can uplift today." Like Alex, many students experience a kind of awakening at the debilitating nature of stereotypes both in relation to other people as well as for their own humanity. An obsession with the idea of one story obliterates our capacity to embrace the complexity of identity. To counter the threat of this pitfall, educators must be vigilant to the lure of the single story. Even when the narrative meets the needs of a particular learning goal (or our limited time to plan), we must research multiple and alternative perspectives. Certainly the arts are useful tools in this endeavor, as there are countless works of art that tell the stories of different moments in time, regions, and people.

Learning to Research: Leaning Outward

As students practice their researching stance, they not only gain a greater critical awareness of the ways in which power shapes our stories, but also practice a newfound agency in reimagining, constructing, and sharing counternarratives. Using their artwork as a tool to disrupt stereotypical, biased, inaccurate, or incomplete perspectives, students lean outward to help others see people within a wider and more nuanced context.

Critical consumers and producers: Artists play important roles in our society as they produce new ways of seeing the world. The artist Mark Addison Smith began his bathroom wall art project in the stall of a truck-stop bathroom in Louisiana. Confronted with scrawled slurs about people who were gay, Smith's curiosity was piqued. Over the course of several years, he documented the writing on the bathroom walls in rest stops across the country. As he critically analyzed what he found, his research revealed patterns within the content and style of these bathroom confessions and condemnations. Turning what were often derogatory statements on their head, Smith transformed some of the found lettering from a men's bathroom stall in Illinois into a new typeface that celebrated gay love. Printed on vinyl stickers, Smith returned his new typeface to the source location in Illinois to write new, affirming messages in his stylized font. Moving from critical consumer to producer, Smith used his research to alter hate-filled texts into visually provocative imagery.

While Smith's artwork doesn't rely on the format of an altered book, his process parallels that of students who research texts in their quest to manipulate them. In conducting the basic research necessary to choose, engage with, and alter a book, students practice the skills of both critically consuming and producing knowledge. Reflecting on how he merged the timeline activity into an altered book, Jose-Manuel described how his attempt to get to know the community of African American Christian people within his neighborhood started with research in a bookstore: "[A]ctually the book found me, so I went into a bookstore that is in the neighborhood. It's a very small bookstore and one of the persons in the community wrote about the community . . . called *Church Girls* . . . the bookstore owner told me the whole story about the lady who did that research and how she wanted to make [known] the voices of these women fighting during the civil rights era and organizing around churches . . . So I thought like that was a perfect resource." After reading the book, Jose-Manuel photocopied images of people who used to live in his neighborhood from *Church Girls* and layered them onto a timeline that he then inserted into a Bible. A self-described nonreligious person, Jose-Manuel found that creating his altered book shifted his understanding of the role of religion in his neighbors' lives. From this perspective, his altered book served to visually humanize a religious text for someone who had never felt any connection to those who practiced organized religion.

Visualizing stories: Images tie our stories and abstract concepts to real-life objects and experiences. This is why we use metaphors to convey complex thoughts and why we grab a pen and a cocktail napkin to diagram an idea. When we give concrete form to ephemeral, theoretical, or emotional knowledge, we make it real in a way that we can hold. Artists and educators know this well. It is why we sketch out ideas and why we create visual presentations. When students create visual timelines, they make the relationships between events easier to see. We can start to see how one event or rising belief might influence another. Perhaps most importantly, as we create our own visual timelines and altered books, we can locate ourselves within complex histories, especially those that might have once seemed unrelated to our own experiences.

The artworks students create in class offer opportunities to make patterns and connections more readily apparent in their study of history. For example, one student created a timeline related to her school community that focused simply on how private and independent schools in New York City have approached co-ed versus single-sex education. Her simple line drawing included color-coded dots that demarcated the year each independent school was founded and whether the school was for boys only, girls only, or co-ed. In pulling out this one aspect of this community's history, her timeline visualized a particular story about historical views of gender and education. Taking a radically different approach, another student repeatedly typed the phrase "when you walk a/long long distance/you are tired" on a long roll of receipt tape. The sometimes overlapping words—for which one could not easily identify a starting point—gave viewers the sense of exhaustion and perseverance she heard in her conversations with people in transitional housing as she learned about the cycles of homelessness many face. In her attempts to build a relationship with people involved in a running club for adults in transitional housing, this poetic and abstract timeline served to visualize a particular kind of history rarely accounted for in conventional formats.

Sharing alternatives and counternarratives: Linda Tuhiwai Smith writes that "[t]o hold alternative histories is to hold alternative knowledges."[19] When we realize that the stories we have been taught about socially constructed identities are not the only stories, our awareness of identity expands. As students work to creatively alter a book, they are forced to stretch beyond the words on the page to include other ideas. In doing so, they are left with a visible reminder of how counternarratives can change not just what we know, but how we know it. What was once a text is now a work of art; their alterations have changed the very medium of their message.

To alter their books, students engage in research about both what the original text says and how they want to manipulate it. In her efforts to better understand and share some of the experiences of English language learners, one student altered a book on the history of immigrants in the United States. By cutting out and redacting portions of the text, creating flaps that open to reveal additional text, and layering in her own handwritten words and collaged imagery, the student transformed the history told within the text. Through the art that emerges from the book, she offered a counternarrative that highlighted the ways in which many immigrant communities were (and are still) forced—often against their own wishes—to learn English in a move driven by capitalist and assimilationist motives. Manipulating the original text to tell an all-too-often hidden story enabled the student to consider a different way of understanding the experiences of English language learners. From within the text itself, a new reading unfolds.

In one of my conversations with a veteran teacher, she quietly relayed a story about a colleague who led a social studies lesson where she dressed her elementary students in a store-bought, generic Native American–style headdress for individual photographic portraits. In our discussion, the veteran teacher, who I had also had as a student, conveyed her dismay in hushed but hurt tones. To contradict the seemingly obvious stereotypes that were conveyed through her colleague's lesson, this veteran teacher brought in images, artworks, and stories of contemporary native people in all forms of attire. While she was not in a position to directly confront her colleague, she researched more nuanced information to hopefully dispel some of the biases she knew had been taught in the room next door. Unfortunately, I do not think this is an isolated story. Yet, with a stance toward a more critical capacity to researching our multiple stories, we could certainly design lessons that engage with identity in a more textured, layered, and complex manner.

CHAPTER 5

Connecting Stance

When we choose to love, we choose to move against fear, against alienation and separation. The choice to love is a choice to connect, to find ourselves in the other.[1]

—bell hooks

THE LAST DAY

Students spread out around the room on the last day to set up their final collaborative art projects. Leena hangs a mobile with small paper circles hanging from colorful string; each circle contains a drawing made by someone in her neighborhood who responded to her prompt, "What do you love about this block?" Olivia pulls out a hand-collaged plate she created with images of food on one side and the recipes she had learned by preparing a meal with someone she met at a church function. Ben removes a black-and-white photograph from a plastic sleeve that includes two images of young children—his own and a colleague's—juxtaposed to illustrate his own growing awareness of his role as a teacher for other people's children. Near the computer, Krisia tests out the video she made—a short film about her changing understanding of silence as defined by the people in the deaf community she has come to know. Charles squeezes through the door wearing a giant pink boa sculpted out of wood and inspired by his time getting to know people in the drag community. Jackie unfolds a quilt made of patched drawings and fabrics sketched and selected by young people in a workshop she led. Finally, Jose-Manuel unfurls two large-scale welcome banners he designed based on conversations he had with members of the Harlem church community about how to project their openness to the neighborhood.

After students have time to look closely at each other's artworks, we spend the rest of this last class sharing reflections from the final project. We gather around Florence's watercolor; it's an image of two apartment buildings—one old brownstone and one new glass and steel structure—with the words "no single storiez" strung like prayer flags between the buildings. Florence tells us how she began her project in hopes of getting to know the people who lived around the El Puente Community Center in her neighborhood. Although she had lived near the predominantly Puerto Rican center for over ten years, she had always felt like an outsider, as if she had no connection. As a white transplant to the area, she figured that she would always feel outside. However, during the semester, as she went to public events, met with people, and researched the artwork and history of the El Puente community, her understanding of her own sense of belonging shifted. Talking with people from El Puente, she realized that there was no single story of their experience; many of the issues and values they discussed were similar to those she talked about among her friends. The imagined wall she had seen separating their insider connections from her outsider identity slowly started to disappear.

Next to Florence's painting, Elle had arranged her black-and-white zines. For the previous fifteen weeks, Elle had joined an early-morning running group for people in transitional housing. Although she had her own apartment, she hoped to deepen her understanding of the experience of people without consistent housing. Several times a week, she laced up her running shoes to join the welcome circle that kicked off the group's regular runs. Before starting each day, they always responded to a question posed by someone in the group. One day, Elle asked if she could ask a question and write down people's answers for an art project. As people went around the circle responding to her query to describe something nice about the person next to them, Elle quickly scribbled their answers. She took these replies home and transformed them into small zines. With stitched binding, these slim, photocopied mini-magazines or zines each contained the first names and replies of her running mates. The following week, she distributed them to the other runners. Later, she recalled their reactions:

[T]hey laughed and said that they didn't realize that this was gonna turn into something, they were just like it was just another question . . . they were just shocked that someone was listening to what they were saying in a circle and . . . taking note and that I knew most of their names . . . I think they were just kind of shocked that they were in a piece of artwork and that they were part of a project. I mean, it gives them a sense of community, I mean like this running is already building that community but it's in terms of art they were able to be a part of this bigger thing than themselves and they were like a piece in the bigger picture. I think that always makes you feel more connected.

As buzzwords go, "collaboration" has a pretty strong following, rivaled perhaps by "building community." In education, we expect educators to nurture relationships with students, colleagues, families, and local organizations, often in an effort to foster a feeling of connection. Unfortunately, as is often the case with buzzwords, the specific characteristics of what collaboration and community really look like, let alone how to cultivate them, are rarely discussed. The few times we discuss community building, we often do so without acknowledging the ways in which socially constructed barriers keep people from connecting with each other across differences. Yet, without an ability to connect with people who are different from us, we cannot possibly try to establish caring and reciprocal relationships.

Throughout each of the previous stances—noticing, wondering, researching—I've emphasized the ideas of really seeing people within all of their complexity. As educators practice connecting, they bring all of these stances together to build relationships. These relationships are the bedrock of community; through our connections with people, we can build a deeper understanding of ourselves and the collective work of learning and teaching. Scholar-educator bell hooks has written and spoken extensively about the vital importance of a sense of community among students and teachers; it is core to practicing education as an act of love and freedom. Writing about how to nurture a sense of community within the classroom, hooks notes that "our capacity to generate excitement is deeply affected by our interest in one another, in hearing one another's voices, in recognizing one another's presence."[2] In other words, we need to value what each person brings to the table and to care about their specific ways of being in the world. Embedded in this is the key concept that we must recognize the differences in our identities, and rather than ignore or deny them, use them as points of connection with each other.

For educators, the capacity to connect with students and their families can shift conventional power dynamics to open up new opportunities for learning and teaching—especially about identity. As I've highlighted earlier, teaching and learning about identity asks us all to be vulnerable and to cultivate particular stances in our work with each other. In a variation of what scholar and Youth Radio producer Lissa Soep calls "collegial pedagogy," when we allow students and teachers to learn with and from each other, the learning tends to be more grounded, relevant, and meaningful.[3] This kind of collaborative learning and teaching alters how we interact with each other; both students and teachers are more likely to be invested in each other's mutual growth and development. This creates an ideal context for the often ambiguous, charged, and complicated conversations about identity that we must have if we believe in any real kind of community building.

Highlighting the connective potential of participatory art making, this chapter includes a description of two art activities—*reflection zines* and *collaborative art projects*—that prompt learners to create and reflect on collaborative art in partnership with people of different identities. To do this, we must know who we are—not just our strengths and talents, but also how we are seen by others. We cannot learn with other people if we cannot connect with them; we cannot connect with them if we cannot see ourselves and the relationships we have with those around us. To cultivate a state toward connecting and collaborating, we must engage in a kind of praxis of both working with people and reflecting critically about our actions. As the students in my class explore these ideas, we read scholarship by Paulo Freire, bell hooks, Bill Ayers, Ryan Alexander-Tanner, Korina Jocson, and Brett Cook, who challenge educators to rethink the ways in which we collaborate and work collectively with each other to transform our society.[4] These readings and conversations encourage students to think creatively about how ideas of connection, praxis, and collaboration can extend into their own artwork as well.

LEARNING FROM HOW ARTISTS CONNECT

Part of what makes art such a useful tool for learning and teaching about identity is its capacity to both literally and figuratively connect the dots. Many artists use their artwork to highlight the connections between different identities. At times, this work is very personal; for example, many people refer to Frida Kahlo's intimate paintings of her own life experiences and how she used imagery to narrate connections between those personal identities. At other times, artists use their art to highlight connections between people of different backgrounds, as in Damon Davis's recent photography project, *All Hands on Deck*, which includes photographs of the hands of Ferguson, Missouri, protesters in the aftermath of Michael Brown's murder—hands that were clearly of many different races, genders, and ages. Simply looking at these artworks can help us visualize the ways in which our various identities intersect. When we also consider the reflection and research it takes to create these works of art, we can see how the very process of creating such artwork can invite connections and collaboration.

Take, for example, the project *Border Farm*, initiated by the artist Thenjiwe Nkosi and writer, farm worker, and community organizer Meza Weza. Over the course of many months, Nkosi and Weza collaborated with a group of Zimbabwean migrant farm workers to conceive of, script, and film a short narrative movie about the experiences of crossing the border between South Africa and Zimbabwe. Certainly, as a document, the film produced from the Border Farm project tells stories of people from different regional and cultural backgrounds. It visually connects their stories together for a public audience. However, perhaps more interesting is the way the actual process of making the film required all participants to find connections across their multiple identities. To make a film together, participants had to have open and honest conversations about how they related to each other. As an artist with South African citizenship, formal academic training, and access to a car and funding for the project, in addition to being the daughter of one black and one white parent, Nkosi's identities corresponded with greater social power than the migrant farm workers with whom she collaborated—many of whom had no official work visas, little formal education, and who were largely poor. To even begin to make a work of art together, the group had to discuss these very different identities and find connections if they were to trust each other enough to create a substantial project. Without those connections, there could be no real collaboration; the final film is testament to their ability to build community across different identities.

Collaborative works of art can also serve as concrete reminders of what might be possible if we could figure out how to connect and work together because of, or in spite of, our differences. In the fall of 2016, the artist Sita Kuratomi Bhaumik worked in collaboration with piñata makers (Piñatas Las Morenitas Martínez, Iván Padilla Mónico, and Little Piñata Maker), muralists (Cece Carpio), youth activists (Young Girls on the Rise), musicians (La Pelanga), and chefs (People's Kitchen Collective and Norma Listman), to develop a work of interactive art entitled *Estamos contra el muro/We Are Against the Wall*. The multifaceted project centered on a wall of tissue-paper-covered papier-mâché bricks crafted by a professional piñata maker and filled with devalued Mexican pesos and hot sauce packets. Built to divide an entire community gallery space, the wall became a kind of canvas for community members to graffiti with their thoughts about the proposed wall between the United States and Mexico. After several weeks, and to a soundtrack of migration-themed songs and a menu of typical border foods, visitors attended a special community demolition party where people had a chance to take a swing at the piñata wall until it came crashing down. Laden with symbolism, this project highlights how collaborative art projects can be sites to bring together people from multiple backgrounds to reenvision reality. In creating a work of art that demonstrates what it might look like to deconstruct the walls between us, these artists show us that such border crossing is, in fact, possible. In other words, the artwork makes the imagined real.

As these examples show, the process of creating works of art about our identities and the connections between them can provide both the makers and the viewers with a space for identifying connections and working collaboratively. To practice a connecting stance, the first activity in this chapter—reflection zines—emphasizes the need to turn inward to reflect on our own identities in order to connect with others. Just as Nkosi and her colleagues had to navigate the power dynamics that existed between them in order to build the trust necessary to work together, the reflection zines ask us to think carefully about our own identities. The second activity—collaborative art—challenges participants to actually create a real work of art with people with whom they might not typically interact. As a culminating activity, collaborative art making requires participants to practice all of the stances as they seek to work together across our different identities. Considering how we connect with people, the writer Alice Walker asks, "How do you wish to meet new people? By sharing recipes, and cooking and eating dinners together, by learning their medicines and dances and gardening techniques, their wisdom and philosophy; by listening to the sound of their language and trying to learn it? While sharing what you have?"[5] Activities to foster connecting encourage students to consider how they can build authentic and caring relationships with people across our social divisions.

ACTIVITY 1

To practice connecting emergent ideas, assumptions, and realizations, reflection zines provide a useful format for turning inward to better understand our own identities.

Reflection Zines

Often crafted out of a single sheet of office printer paper and photocopied cheaply, zines have long been popular for their ease of production and distribution. While their history dates back to the pamphlets and science fiction "fanzines" created in the early twentieth century, zines became increasingly popular in the 1970s and 80s as copy machines became more accessible. Favored by subcultures such as the punk and riot grrrl movements, zines typically feature text, drawings, and collaged imagery pieced together on topics ranging from music and food to politics and identity. Today, one can find zine festivals, zine exchanges, and zine sections of bookstores and art stores around the world. Created with a handmade, do-it-yourself aesthetic, zines tend to appeal to both professional and novice artists and writers as a tool to readily create and share ideas. The accessibility of this art form makes it an ideal format for documenting and processing ongoing self-reflection.

Although I introduce this activity here in the chapter about the connecting stance, you can incorporate variations of this activity into any conversation about identity. The most basic version of a reflection zine begins with a single sheet of paper. With a series of folds, students can transform the paper into a palm-sized, multipage booklet. Depending on the focus of each reflection zine, I have often offered specific prompts, guidelines, or constraints to direct students' creativity, such as responding to a suggested reading, quote, or image or creating a visual representation of their thoughts (for additional ideas, see suggestions in the sidebar "Reflection Zines"). With encouragement to create zines in a fashion that makes sense to their individual processes of reflection, the final products tend to vary wildly. Some students create zines using only found photographs and drawings clipped from magazines or newspapers to convey their thoughts. Others stick with text, experimenting with different typed or handwritten fonts, redacting words from texts to create new meaning, or writing poetry and prose as they analyze their own reactions. Still others juxtapose the two, layering text atop images; connecting words with lines, arrows, or interlocking circles; or illustrating entire narratives. No matter the approach, each zine offers a visual document of the creator's thoughts and a tool with which to continue analyzing them.

Reflection Zines

Share the history of zines: For many students, learning that people with limited formal art training have used zines in social and cultural movements can free them from any creative inhibitions. Share examples from a wide variety of styles and formats, from zines that are simple ballpoint pen drawings and photocopies to more elaborate mixed media and professionally printed zines.

Introduce simple art techniques: Using example zines and either online or in-person demonstrations, describe accessible art techniques such as simple pen or pencil drawings, magazine and news collages, and pop-up book methods (i.e., flaps, pull tabs). Encourage students to try different approaches until they find a style that best enables them to convey their thoughts; this will likely be very different for each student.

Encourage critical reflection: Direct students to identify connections, questions, surprises, and key takeaways as they try to build relationships with community members. Provide readings that can expand their thinking; ask them to include resonant quotes in their zines. Encourage them to use the zines to reflect on their own thinking and to analyze their thoughts using a combination of text and imagery.

Establish regularity: Design a structure for students to develop a habit of reflection with their zines. This may include in-class work time or set deadlines for sharing zines with with peers or with the facilitator.

Practical Considerations for Implementation

Emphasize simplicity: Perhaps one of the greatest strengths of the zine format is its lack of pretense. Unlike other art forms, zines are not intimidating to make. They do not require expensive materials or technical expertise. While an artistically talented student might bring a level of technical skill and beauty to these artworks, even those students who claim to "not know how to draw a straight line" can create something meaningful and engaging. The format of a small book creates a familiar template for telling the story of one's thoughts. Educators who facilitate this activity should emphasize these characteristics of the zine by sharing examples, highlighting the do-it-yourself aesthetic, and setting clear guidelines that allow participants to use simple materials if they choose. Zines allow us to celebrate the hastily drawn stick figure as much as the precise representative portrait, and educators should support a full range of responses based on learners' artistic choices and experiences.

Focused prompts: When first introducing reflection zines, provide specific prompts to spark critical analyses of identity. Such prompts might mirror classroom discussions or relate to shared readings. For example, you might ask learners to illustrate their thoughts before, during, and after a conversation about identity or to create a collage of found images that remind them of a particular reading. Other prompts might take inspiration from the book format of a zine to ask learners to narrate a story within its pages. For example, students could tell a story of the first time they became aware of a particular element of their identity or about a time when they felt connected (or not) to someone because of (or in spite of) an aspect of their identity. Zine reflection prompts can also focus on artistic constraints such as limited color palettes (only shades of gray), word choices (only adjectives), art materials (only ballpoint pen), source material (only newspaper), time for completion (only fifteen minutes), and so on. After experimenting with a variety of prompts and constraints, you can gradually expand the options based on the needs of each learner to allow for open-ended reflection zines.

Make it a habit: To encourage participants to develop a regular habit of reflection, you should build a routine of creating reflection zines. The artist, writer, illustrator, and educator Lynda Barry writes about the importance of daily drawing with a timer to build a strong habit.[6] Because zines are relatively simple to make, you might require frequent zine responses at set times throughout a class or in reaction to weekly readings or daily discussions.

The idea is to enable participants to think of visually recording and reflecting on their thoughts almost every day.

ACTIVITY 2

Building on all of the previous activities, this culminating activity encourages students to use all of the stances they have practiced to lean outward as they collaborate with people to make a work of art.

Collaborative Art Projects

All of the collaborative art projects I have been involved with as a collaborator have been simultaneously transformative and challenging. In their hardest moments, they have forced me to stretch in uncomfortable ways as I came to see my blind spots, limitations, and assumptions about my relationships with other people. And in their best moments, they have taught me to see connections to people I had thought were so different from me— connections that changed how I understood who I am in the world. By definition, collaborative art requires the active participation of more than one person to create a work of co-constructed art. Typical examples include murals created by community groups, ethnodrama, forum theater, community choreographed dance performances, and multi-musician jam sessions. Collaborative art is as much about a *process* of making art that encourages participants to build relationships and nurture a sense of connectedness as it is about an aesthetically engaging *product*. Yet stating that a work of art is collaborative and actually making a work of art that is collaborative can be remarkably different tasks.

The collaborative art project is the final activity I assign in my courses. Building on the connections they have nurtured, the assumptions they have revealed, and the understandings they have gained, the students create a work of art with one or more people from the community they have started to get to know. I give very few parameters in terms of materials or techniques, only that they create a work that relates to the connections they have come to see across different identities (see the guidelines I suggest in the sidebar "Collaborative Art Projects"). Many students return to some of the people they met when they created their interview portraits or attended public events.

Relying on varying degrees of collaboration, students create works of art about how they experience identity with other people. Often their projects involve some form of creative exchange whereby a student invites community members to contribute ideas, responses to a question, drawings, recipes, or images that the student then transforms into a work of art. For example, Jack's collaborative work emerged from responses he solicited from people in his neighborhood to the question, "What do you like about this community?" He then turned their replies into paper bricks with which he constructed a wall of interlocking comments. Other collaborative projects involve mutual exchange. Another student, a paraprofessional of Dominican descent, Lisette was interested in deepening her understanding of a Jewish colleague's culture. Over several conversations, they realized that each of their cultural communities shared a similar relationship to specific kinds of bread. For her collaborative art project, Lisette exchanged recipes and loaves of bread—she brought *pan de agua*[7] and her colleague brought a loaf of challah. Lisette created a book to document their shared lunch and favorite bread recipes. Jarin, a psychology student who had been raised with little exposure to the Bangladeshi side of her family was interested in learning more about the Bangladeshi community in her neighborhood. During the other activities, she realized that the language barrier she experienced formed a surprising barrier at times to relating with people. Additionally, she learned that "language was very important to the community since they fought for their language and wanted to preserve it." She used her collaborative art project to reflect on this through a series of very short interviews she conducted with people she met in the neighborhood. She spliced the interviews together— interviews in both Bengali and English—into a short audio recording. As she played it for our class, she noted that she had thought about translating parts for those of us who did not speak Bengali, but decided against it because she realized that the sense of confusion and desire to understand that we might feel would echo her own experience.

Collaborative Art Projects

Determine level of collaboration: Before developing any project, students must determine if they have established a strong enough relationship with one or more people from the community they have been getting to know. Truly co-created projects require a deep sense of trust between collaborators. If students have not built a strong connection with someone, then they might consider a project that requires less focused collaboration and less commitment from collaborators. Such projects may involve small acts of participation (i.e., drawings, interviews, found objects, etc.) rather than deeper mutual commitment (i.e., a co-created work of art). Alternatively, if students have not connected with people or had the opportunity for any collaborative work, they should focus only on creating work that critically reflects *their own* areas of growth and understanding. These works will be introspective rather than collaborative.

Ask permission; invite collaboration: Once they have decided on an appropriate level of collaboration, given their relationships with community members, students should graciously ask permission and invite potential collaborators to create a work of art. No one should be directed or coerced into participation.

Be clear about project goals: When inviting collaborators, students should clearly describe their own motivations, goals, and expectations. To avoid dominating a project, students must seek to understand collaborators' motivations, goals, and expectations as well. Establish clarity about the amount of time, effort, form of engagement, and imagined final outcome (including transparency about who will see the work) at the outset.

Match the art methods to the message: Consider what ideas the audience should take away from viewing the artwork. Will the art encourage them to see people differently or to question socially constructed barriers? Will the artwork challenge stereotypes or reveal human complexity? Use explorations of other works of art to identify art methods that can most effectively communicate to audiences. Metaphor, juxtaposition, humor, personal narrative, and symbolism can pair with any art materials to create evocative works of art.

Practical Considerations for Implementation

Discuss types of collaboration: Anyone who has been assigned a group project knows that collaboration comes in various degrees and formats. When introducing the collaborative art project, as an educator, you should discuss the many ways in which we can work together with people to create a work of art. For example, for some students, this task seems manageable: they have created significant bridges with people in the community they've gotten to know and are eager to create something together. Take, for example,

Jocelyn's final project. Fashioned out of a shoebox with holes for each finger puppet to stand in, Jocelyn's "Action Burger" game presented a very different kind of project. Intrigued by her younger brother's interests in video games, Jocelyn had started the semester hoping to build a relationship with a gaming community. As an international student from Taiwan, Jocelyn wanted to connect with her little brother from afar, so after an online search, she found a gaming community of young people who met regularly at a restaurant called Action Burger. Jocelyn spent several months meeting the young gamers, who quickly taught her the rules of several popular games (such as Super Smash Bros.) and welcomed her into their network. For her final project, she wanted to create something to capture the interactive nature of her engagement with her new comrades and to honor them. She created small puppets of some of the Action Burger regulars and planned to bring her homemade stage to share with the group. She had even made a finger puppet of herself to include in the set.

For other students and teachers, the collaboration can be even more open-ended and function as an exchange of ideas and creativity. One former student, Mateo, describes a regular collaborative art project he initiated with a group of students and parents in his school: "A couple of times I've had parents come and we painted. We did free painting or we did circle painting or we did big collaborative pieces starting with dot paintings. Dots and circles and everybody starts working around and they like what they produce and they keep going and going and going and going until something emerges." This kind of collaboration requires significant trust among all, but often results in deeper relationships among those who participate.

For some students, this final task might not be possible; perhaps they have only scratched the surface in getting to know people or have not established a strong enough sense of trust with them. I encourage them to create a work of art that can be an invitation to rethink common assumptions and biases about identity. Do not force a collaborative project on anyone who is not ready to build mutually trusting relationships. Students who have chosen this alternative option have created self-reflective works of art that portray their own changing consciousness about identity. For example, Max illustrated a self-portrait with a third eye, highlighting his desire to add extra awareness in his relationships with others. While his work was not directly collaborative in nature, it drew upon his experiences learning about Polish culture in his neighborhood and sought to encourage others to develop a third eye towards how they view themselves in the world.

Moving from directing to facilitating: Often students are quite excited about this project and start imagining what they might invite people to create with them. They dream up ideas for collaborative photography projects to document a neighborhood or cowritten comic books to describe a migration experience. However, as they get to know the people in their chosen community group, these project ideas always start to unravel. As they meet people, talk to them, learn about their histories, and contextualize their experiences, those initial project ideas suddenly appear one dimensional. The revision begins, ideally in conversation with people from the community they are working with. While I often refer to this part of the collaboration as the "muddy part" of the process, it is also the most important, as it signifies the shift from directing a project to facilitating one. In facilitating, students practice building relationships, consensus, and mutual understanding to create a work of art.

Name and critique the power dynamics: Collaborative art projects bring people together to create something across their different social identities. However, we are not absolved from thinking critically about this work. The strongest, most engaging works of collaborative art are those in which the participants actively discuss, critique, and hopefully challenge the power dynamics associated with their different identities. As bell hooks has written, "[T]o build community requires vigilant awareness of the work we must continually do to undermine all the socialization that leads us to behave in ways that perpetuate domination."[8]

Learning to Connect: Turning Inward

As I've underscored throughout this book, we must create opportunities to turn our stances inward as we learn to connect with people who are somehow different from us. To know others, we must also know ourselves. This requires diligent critical reflection about our various social identities and how those identities shift based on where we are, who we are with, and what we are doing. This is not work we are often taught in school; yet, the work of reflecting on how we move through the world can enable us to positively transform the relationships we have with each other.

Creating space to reflect: Good educators know that constant reflection helps us continue to improve our practice; the same goes for learning and teaching about identity. Because our various identities are always shifting and evolving, we need to develop tools to regularly analyze how we understand ourselves in relation to other people. Talking about the importance of self-awareness, poet Sonia Sanchez reflected: "I cannot tell the truth about anything unless I confess being a student, growing and learning something new every day."[9] She continued, "The more I learn, the clearer my view of the world becomes."[10] Unfortunately, this kind of reflection takes time and effort. Not unlike dental flossing, it is something we must build into our regular routines. Reflection zines can provide a space to remind us to reflect. Because of their portability, accessibility, and simplicity, they can be an unintimidating format for documenting our thinking. It takes little effort to find a sheet of paper, fold it to fit in your hand or pocket, and sketch or jot ideas within its small pages.

Within their zines, student reflections merge personal anecdotes, questions, quotes from readings, snippets of conversations, and ideas for their current and future work as educators. When reviewing student zines, I learn more about how they are making sense of their experiences building relationships with people in new communities. They often include thoughts that they might not typically voice in class. For example, one student described how getting to know more about a community outside her typical social spheres was affecting her previous friendships, as they questioned her need to cross socially constructed ethnic and class lines. Another student documented her evolving awareness of her own racial identity as a Latina who looks white and what that might mean for her future students. Other students use their zines to draw lines between course readings and discussions, using the space as a format to continue a train of thought that began in class. As a space to reflect, zines offer an additional tool to encourage the kind of introspective and critical connecting that we must each undertake in order to better understand who we are in relation to each other.

Relating ideas visually: Merging text and drawn or found imagery, zines offer an accessible format for articulating an educator's developing awareness of identity. Often created with the sketchlike feel of stream-of-consciousness art making or personal journaling, zines mirror the process of reflection: they are unfolding, layered, and personal. Artists and educators Arzu Mistry and Todd Elkin have taken the reflection zine further in their *Unfolding Practice* project in which they create accordion-style books to reflect on their teaching and their identities as artists. Describing the process, Mistry notes in an interview, "I'm literally constructing my own thinking. The act of gluing and cutting and printing is a way to make my thoughts into a physical object."[11] Here she captures why these accordion books and other handmade reflection books or zines can be so useful for teaching and learning about identity. When we create opportunities to track our own thinking visually, we can turn our thoughts into physical forms. Turning the pages of these documents allows us to see our own thoughts anew, to analyze and dissect how we comprehend our own identities and our relationships.

As one student, Leena, hypothesized in an interview, "The arts aren't always clear-cut and there's not so much a right and wrong, as there is room for interpretation and discussion. I think this is one of the reasons the arts are useful when it comes to learning about identity, community, and culture because they're topics that can be a little confusing and not quite clear-cut and straightforward . . . the arts allow you to reflect back on ideas." Leena's sentiment highlights how the concepts of identity can be complicated for many people to process in linear, formal, or direct ways. Sometimes we need an alternative access point to enter our own thoughts. Creating art can help us find this, especially when we are not caught up in the perfection of getting a work of art just right. Zines, with their do-it-yourself aesthetic, are the ideal format for exploring our own reactions and understandings about who we are in relation to each other.

Tracking evolving reflections: As visual documents of students' critical analyses of their experiences, reflection zines offer a record that can track their evolving understandings. At the end of a semester or workshop, the zines that each student creates tell the unfolding stories of their own thinking. Unlike rich classroom discussion for which there is no remaining physical trace, reflection zines enable students to capture fleeting ideas and to attach them to text and imagery for later consultation. In this way, reflection zines can help students translate the complex reflections they have about identity into something concrete. As Gloria Anzaldúa writes, "Nothing happens in the 'real' world unless it first happens in the images in our heads."[12] Zines help students move inner thoughts into visual records; from there, those thoughts can be sculpted into action. When I asked one former student, Alex, what resonated with her from her experience in my course, she immediately described the reflection zines:

I loved it! You have to do [it] every week but I thought that it was a great way . . . it was a really nice way to respond visually and pull out different quotes and then just to see that gradual process of adding more paper on and seeing it grow and being able to look back and reflect on what you have written the week prior or sort of getting inside from that. I just remember looking at and visually what I was thinking about that day, about what I had drawn in response to a reading and then I'd want to read it over again. It was always like a curiosity on what was I thinking.

Learning to Connect: Leaning Outward

A connecting stance asks us to practice reaching for some shared humanity with people. It requires us to intentionally search for some commonality (no matter how small) that will forge a link (no matter how tenuous) between people. Once we identify a connection, we are suddenly no longer strangers or others. From those initial ties, we can start to find more. As students seek to create artwork with people they did not previously know, they see connections where they had thought there were none. Through making artwork with or in response to interactions with new people, those links multiply, sometimes so deeply that the initial link can become a bond. Through their collaborative art projects, students learn key skills to nurture the connections between people.

Establishing mutual trust: As Jasmin, another former student, later joked in our interview, "Nothing says loving like collaboration." To agree to work with someone else to create a work of art is to take a risk in another person, to trust in a mutual relationship. She continued, "To collaborate with somebody would be like the next step after all of this inquiry and this like comfort zone and discomfort zone finding. 'Cause when you find someone's discomfort zone, you got two options; you can constantly press that button because you're being a jerk and you want to make them uncomfortable, or you can use that as an alert to yourself like, 'Oh wait, I forgot she doesn't like pickles. Let me not ever mention pickles right now' . . . So yeah, the collaboration part is big." Since much of the work of collaborative art projects requires people of different identities to be creative together, mutual trust is the linchpin of a successful project. It is the key to allow people to work through difficult creative decisions, to foster a sense of connectedness and coherence, to imagine wild possibilities, and to implement creative work that meets the expectations of all those involved. It is also elusive, slippery, and nearly impossible to pin down on a timeline, curriculum, or project proposal. Yet, without a sense of trust among the participants of a collaborative art project, the entire endeavor risks inadvertently harming the very goals of cross-identity bridge building. To nurture trust, students must let go of the individual sense of ownership we so often bring to art making and prepare for collective ownership of ideas, artworks, and the credits coming from that work. This process asks students to focus on the act of collaboration as much as on the act of making a work of art, ultimately shifting everyone's focus to the relationships between participants. Not unlike the love that Jasmin named, collaboration asks us to cross the social barriers that divide us to invest in each other in the hopes that we can create something richer, more nuanced, and more creative together.

Learning with *people*: Reflecting about her experiences learning and teaching about identity in the arts, novice teacher Leena recalled two major takeaways that she planned to incorporate into her classroom: the first was "the idea of not filling children's heads, as if they were empty vessels, but instead remembering students have ideas and contributions and that we should build knowledge together." And second, "remembering that students come to each place with their own understandings and experiences, and that as a teacher it is important to be mindful of this and honor what they know." The collaborative art projects provide an opportunity for students to put this concept into action when they shift to co-learning with participants to develop a work of art. Educators involved in collaborative art projects are no longer the primary experts leading participants through a preconceived art project; instead, they are often facilitators who learn along *with* participants. In these spaces where people create works of art collaboratively, educators have as much to learn as the participants. Likewise, in order for a collaborative art project to be successful, the participants must also share the responsibility of educating; their expertise is equally important. Unlike conventional learning sites, collaborative art projects employ less hierarchical leadership roles to ensure that all participants are empowered to contribute. This shared learning alters conventional modes of communication between people of different identities: those in social positions of power must practice listening to those from less dominant social identities. As people from different identities learn more about each other, their understanding of the social dynamics of identity deepen and expand.

Looking back on this, Avery, a former student offers some advice in our interview after the class: "I think people need to know how receptive people are. You also don't have to know all the answers, but you have to want to ask questions and listen to them and not put a judgment on them." Thinking about her approach to making art with people also dovetailed with how she was rethinking curriculum development and teaching: "That was so hopeful and very important for me in thinking about curriculum development, about where do we pause and let there be a discussion. When do I stop being the leader of where this is going and give it room to go to where it needs to go to for them and having that kind of flexibility?" Questions such as Avery's are fundamental to consider if we are to veer from telling people what to do to figuring it out together.

Documenting the connection: Obviously, collaborative art projects provide participants with a task that results in a tangible creation. While the importance of discussions about identity should not be underestimated, they are ephemeral. Furthermore, they occasionally frustrate people who are eager to move their conceptual ideas about cross-identity relationships into action. Where thoughtful conversations about who we are in relation to each other constantly twist and turn into tangents and new topics, collaborative art projects are goal oriented. They ask us to make something together. The resulting works of art then serve as artifacts or evidence of our engagement with each other. In many ways, these final projects are the action part of Freirean calls for a praxis approach to learning. We reflect on the intersecting identities among people from different social groups, we collaborate to create a work of art, and the resulting artwork is testament to our relationship and a point of departure for more conversations. Jasmin underscored this idea in our interview: collaboration works because participants create something "that exists because of" each person involved.

Creating and sustaining relationships: In our final reflections on these collaborative art projects, many students describe initial nervousness in initiating a project followed by some trial-and-error moments as they developed a collaborative project with people across different identities. Despite their trepidation, most students describe a series of aha moments as they work with other people. Reflecting on her experience getting to know a group of gamers and creating the Action Burger puppet theater, Jocelyn laughed at her own realizations. She shared how she thought she would never find much that would resonate with her among a group of young video game players; she assumed their interests and modes of communication would be too different for them to really relate to each other. Yet, here she was on the last day of class describing how she planned to keep meeting with the group because she really enjoyed their company and was learning to like the games they played.

Delilah, a veteran teacher who had created a postcard project with people living in the South Bronx (a neighborhood in New York City), recounted her experiences in an interview several months after her project:

> It was challenging trying to figure out how I was going to connect with people who were absolute strangers. I'm not really somebody who tends to reach out to strangers in that way so I guess that was good for me. People were pretty warm and open and willing to share so . . . I left it open to people to make postcards that shared something that they wanted people outside the community to know about them, perhaps things that they believe that others had misconceptions about. And people seemed pretty willing to share.

That said, Delilah had some bumps along the way:

> I did [the project] on a few different days in a few areas of the South Bronx. First I tried going to businesses because it seemed like I'd have a captive audience that way, but it didn't necessarily work out that well because people were trying to work or they didn't—they didn't necessarily come from the area. So I wound up going to a couple galleries and there were people who were willing to share at the galleries and I think that being from an art background they were more willing to explore . . . I tried a laundromat. That did not work out at all! How are people going to write when they're trying to fold their laundry? So then I wound up going to a community center. And that worked out a lot better. There were a lot more people available and they were willing to share since they're also coming from a place where they want to connect with others.

In addition to learning more about the businesses, galleries, community centers, and laundromats in the neighborhood, Delilah also reconsidered how people interact with space.

In the end, Delilah, who was from a different area of the Bronx, felt that the project didn't seem as challenging as she had anticipated. She realized she had a lot in common with people from the neighborhood she was coming to know: "I think if you're from [any neighborhood in] the Bronx, you probably already have this idea that people look at you as if you live in a bad area if they haven't been to the Bronx so I think we all kind of shared this insecurity." When I talked to Delilah after the project, she also reflected on how creating a postcard project with people she hadn't known well contributed to her own growth: "Typically I'm very guarded, especially out in public because you don't know who you're gonna open yourself up to, so I had to constantly remind myself: 'It's ok. It's alright. I know that this is against the grain but it's alright, you can open up to strangers. What's the worst that happens? There's all these other people around' . . . reminding myself that they're people like anybody else and you know the people that I know now were at one point strangers."

⁂

On that last day of class, in addition to a sense of excitement in sharing their final works, I often sense a touch of relief that everyone has survived each activity of the community engagement project. It's not unlike a deep exhale. Often, we laugh about this together: "You made it!" I joke, "We didn't lose anyone!" And they admit that it wasn't as bad as they had anticipated. Though they are quick to remind me that it wasn't easy either. This I understand. To reach across the socially constructed barriers that delineate who can interact with whom in our society is jarring. Add to that the challenge of creating art to share publicly with classmates and sometimes a wider audience, and I have no doubt that I have asked much of the students in my class. Yet, we should be asking this much of each other. Reflecting on making artwork, playwright and poet Ntozake Shange reminds us that "[b]eing an artist is a scary thing. When they say you take your life in your hands or write a poem like you took your life in your hands or say a line like it's the last breath you'll ever use or jump in the air until you feel like you're gonna reach Jupiter, we say things like that; we really mean it."[13] I'd argue that there's a similar sense of risk in trying to build bridges with people you have been taught not to know. But the risks are worth it.

CHAPTER 6

Reflections and Stances in Action

This is precisely the time when artists go to work. There is no time for despair, no place for self-pity, no need for silence, no room for fear. We speak, we write, we do language. That is how civilizations heal. I know the world is bruised and bleeding, and though it is important not to ignore its pain, it is also critical to refuse to succumb to its malevolence. Like failure, chaos contains information that can lead to knowledge—even wisdom. Like art.[1]

—Toni Morrison

Three years ago, I sat in the audience as four alumni of the "Identity, Community, and Culture in Art Education" course presented their reflections at a national conference. Listening to these former students, now teachers in schools and museums across New York City, I was riveted by how they described their own unfurling consciousness and how their experiences using art to learn about identity had changed their own pedagogies. Nowhere else, in no other subject area, they argued, are educators and young people afforded the opportunities for complexity, ambiguity, flexibility, and openness that are possible through the arts and that are necessary for teaching about, within, and across identity difference. The arts, they argued, are where we can truly delve into the nature of identity, power, and privilege in our society and, more importantly, where we can actively work for understanding across difference. As people in the audience reacted with excitement and curiosity about how educators could use the arts to better understand themselves, their students, and their communities, I realized that there might be a wider audience for this kind of conversation.

In many ways, this book, and the research on which it is based, emerged from that moment. Interviewing alumni of the courses I've taught has enabled me to learn again from their insights on what it means to get to know people and to know ourselves—and how the arts can support this work. In the previous chapters, I've described a set of stances that students have practiced in our efforts to build relationships with people who we might once have called strangers. In doing so, I've highlighted how these stances require both inward and outward work, and I have pointed to some of the ways in which students noted their own growth in practicing their stances. As I look back on their reflections, several overarching takeaways—some internal and others more external—emerge that underscore the kind of learning that working on these stances can inspire.

TAKEAWAYS: TURNING INWARD

Given how much critical self-reflection the stances ask of students, it is no wonder that many alumni of the course noted profound changes in how they see themselves and the ways in which they connect (or don't) with other people. Turning inward allowed students to challenge themselves to stretch beyond their comfort zones, to learn more about their own perceptions, and to refresh their sense of agency as educators seeking to connect with students and communities.

Getting Comfortable with Being Uncomfortable

A running theme through every open-ended interview I had with alumni of my course was their realization that they needed to become comfortable with being uncomfortable if they wanted to build genuine relationships with their students and communities. In getting to know people outside their typical social circles, students acknowledged that this willingness to lean into discomfort was their ticket to growth and connection. As one former student, Jasmin, described, "People may not realize that some of the things they think about other people are offensive until they really dig deeply enough. Until they're like, comfortable enough to express it. Until they have a conversation with a person that feels similar or different about it. What helps me get to that place is, preparing myself to be uncomfortable." For some, this move was compounded by their self-professed shyness; yet, as they challenged themselves to reach out of their comfort zone, they could feel a sense of expansion in their understanding. In her interview, Shannon, another former student, shared her sincere fear of completing the outward-leaning assignments: "I think maybe I'm a little bit of the shyer introvert side. There was also the fear of embarrassing myself, embarrassing them, the fear of doing something wrong that would be disrespectful." However, she noted, "It was real—it worked. It was really great but, wow, that was uncomfortable."

For every student, the discovery that they must embrace the sense of discomfort led to a newfound awareness of how the desire to remain comfortable reinforces the socially constructed divisions between people. When, as Jackie, another student, imagined, we open the door of our own comfortable rooms and are brave enough to step outside, that's when we can encounter new ideas and perspectives that—though at times scary or disorienting—encourage us grow and build connections with people. Reflecting on her experience, Jennifer, a former student, said that she had to get used to "feeling like a stranger . . . It was intimidating, but I learned a lot from that experience. Even just noticing how intimidated I was was a learning experience. It kind of made me realize how segregated people are in their daily lives . . . It made me realize that I could go around in my life and have very little interaction with people even if they live right where I live. I hadn't realized that was the case until I went to approach people and it felt really awkward." Olivia echoed this sentiment when she reflected on getting to know a new group of people: "I remember feeling very vulnerable and very unsure of myself, but also knowing that I was supposed to do that, I was supposed to feel that way . . . because the idea was to stretch your boundaries." Stretching—that activity that takes us back to the athletic metaphor of our stances—is a reminder that getting accustomed to being uncomfortable may result in some tenderness and pulling. We may need to warm up to it. However, as every student said, being OK with discomfort is what allows us to reach through the social barriers that separate us from other people and to build real relationships across difference.

Realizing Our Assumptions

Reflecting on their growth in the course, several students used the word "awakening" to describe an expanded sense of themselves. As Jane noted, she experienced "sort of this awakening that I hadn't ever considered my identity and then I hadn't considered what had been constructed inside of me." Through activities that encouraged students to turn inward to critically analyze the ways in which our identities are built through our social environments, many students described a heightened awareness of their own assumptions and biases. Max shared: "I mean just being able to check my own assumptions and check my blind spots and realize the assumptions that I had specifically towards the Polish-American, Polish people in general [the community Max got to know] . . . I definitely learned some things about myself and learned how I could really be aware of my positionality or my privilege or my race, or when I talk about it. When I talk about race, I have to think obviously about what is my position, how am I complacent in certain aspects of racism or gender roles and masculinity." Likewise, another student, Kendra G., saw how her lenses for viewing the world were colored by her own experiences in ways she hadn't anticipated: "I was bringing my own baggage into the project because my dad was in a nursing home and so every nursing home I went into I was like, 'It's so somber and it's just so sad.' That was me, bringing my own baggage and that wasn't the case when I visited one of the nursing homes—it wasn't somber. They were having a grand old time!"

While learning to name our own biases can be unsettling, several students noted the importance of naming our assumptions in order to dismantle them. Leena quietly reflected on how useful it was to articulate her own stereotypes instead of hiding them: "I learned some of the misconceptions I might have about things . . . to look deeper at things and to acknowledge things you might think—judgments or stereotypes you might have about people, because sometimes you might think them but shut them out, but the class taught me that it's OK to acknowledge it and think about why you have it."

As students moved to unravel their biases, they saw themselves as having agency to undo what they had been taught. The assumptions suddenly were breakable. After her experience in the course, Elle noted how "it's weird to say that learning about other people makes you have a stronger sense of identity, but it helps build an understanding of what other people are experiencing and going through." This empathy led many students to focus on the permeability of our assumptions about people. Elle continued, "I need to realize that there's going to be biases no matter what and I have to put those aside." Articulating their misconceptions about people who were somehow different, and then getting to actually listen to and interact with someone while reflecting on the experience, enabled students to chip away, or sometimes shatter, the biases they had previously held. Once those initial biases started to crack, many students described their awareness that perhaps all of their assumptions about other people might be equally flawed.

Seeing Self in New Ways

Reflecting on a moment in class, Kendra T. explained a sudden awareness of her own identity: "I had that epiphany: I think I know who I am gonna be, instead of worrying about what other people think of me, because I worried about that for so long." Kendra shared how she had realized that she had allowed others' perceptions and exceptions to shape her sense of self, and that she now—after meeting new people and reflecting on the experience—had a different sense of control over how she identified herself. Rafael shared a similar kind of shift:

> During that project, I started to question my own identity—like what do I most identify with? And I did find that although I do speak Spanish and I'm definitely a New Yorker, that my heart really is over there on the island [Puerto Rico] and with nature and that's what I really want. And so, during that project I found myself really questioning which part of my identity do I really gravitate towards most. Since then I've heavily leaned towards that more natural way of living and I've done a lot more research on it and I've tried to learn bits of the language that have survived and . . . it makes you think. Not only about learning about other cultures, but then you just start thinking about your own and how diverse it is.

Many students wrote about this in their reflection zines as they processed a deepening awareness of their own sense of self. In meeting new people, they learned to see new parts of themselves.

These realizations about their own identities and values woke up several students to new possibilities for connection with others. Alex described this in our interview: "It was a good awakening, again, just like we have more people that we can meet and involve ourselves with and I think that was something that just shook me a little bit to do that. It's definitely allowed me to think and see things in different ways because we talked so much about it and we, you know, spent months discussing how you deal with or how might you interact with different communities, different cultures, how might you approach that in an open-minded way and accepting way." Like Alex, many students described a more fine-tuned awareness of how they move in the world in relation to other people. Jose-Manuel laughed as he described this sensation: "I have another antenna right now—like a third 'listener' . . . I can't help it right now!"

Along with this, several students described a renewed feeling of purpose in their role as educators who are capable of building genuine relationships with students and communities. Avery mused: "I feel that now I try to think about that more, being around different people will help with that— because if you're only around people who are a part of the same group that share interests or a group of people that you look like it's easy to feel like it normalizes it. I try to be more aware about who I am walking in the world and how that might be affecting other people or what it might represent to other people and I think that's so important—as an educator you're going into spaces where you're trying to create a different environment."

LEANING OUTWARD

Intertwined with the personal takeaways that alumni of my course named were other, more outward-facing, aha moments. As students started to con- nect their learning to their own actions, their views about how they move in the world, the connections they can make, and how they might now approach their teaching began to shift. New possibilities for building com- munity through the arts revealed themselves in their reflections.

Connections to a Community

As students moved out into the world to meet and engage with new people, they developed initial connections that reminded them that such links can come easily with more intentional practice. As they met new people, many students began to see possibilities for connection more frequently, even if they felt it was not their typical way of behaving.

One former student, Delilah, shared her own trepidation and how she overcame it: "Typically I'm very guarded, especially out in public, because you don't know who you're gonna open yourself up to. So I had to con- stantly remind myself, it's ok. It's alright. I know that this is against the grain, but it's alright, you can open up to strangers. What's the worst that happens? . . . reminding myself that they're people like anybody else and you know the people that I know now were at one point strangers." Linking this capacity to connect with strangers to a more nuanced view of her own biases, Kendra T. shared how her previous assumptions had prevented her from trying to connect with some people: "I learned that I shouldn't just judge people just based off what they look like, because even as a person of color, I can learn a lot as well in terms of prejudices and judgment." She continued reflecting on getting to know new people: "That experience [of meeting people in a Jewish community] actually opened my mind that there are people out there that are still welcoming and they will embrace anybody . . . I learned a lot from them about their culture, their history, their religion, what their thoughts were, and how even like my religion and my beliefs actually connected closely with theirs! I actually met someone where we kind of connected. So that was really exciting for me." As strangers became connections and acquaintances, each student's social circle expanded.

For several students—particularly those who chose to get to know their own neighborhood communities—the connections they made profoundly altered their day-to-day experiences. Alex shared how she developed a renewed sense of connection to people: "I guess it's like an openness that's placed back into me. It's not that I was closed off to not wanting to talk with other people, but I think I just felt in my own personality the need not to." She described the pattern of behavior that many of us abide by—especially in large cities: "Don't stop and chat with somebody on the sidewalk." Yet, as she got to know her neighborhood community more, this changed: "I . . . started saying hi to people in my neighborhood and asking how they are doing . . . so that's been a nice way to not be afraid to talk to people, maybe a way of opening or seeing things in a different way that we're all individuals and that it's OK to say hi." Oddly, for many people, saying hi can actually feel quite challenging; yet, as many students noted, when they did, new connections unfolded.

Permission to Talk About Identity

As students shared their key takeaways from their experience in the course, many of them started to think about how to translate what they learned into their own teaching. Given the pervasive silences around talking about our social and cultural identities in schools, several students discussed the importance of feeling confident even addressing identity with students. As

Max stated, the class "gave me permission to talk about issues that I might not have normally talked about" with students. He continued, "I just realized that as an art educator being in the identity class, the permission was given to me to talk about these issues and the confidence to talk about assumptions, especially stereotypes." Based on this confidence, Max initiated a conversation with students in his class the Wednesday after the 2016 election— a conversation that he said was much needed in his school, as it provided students a chance to express their concerns, fears, and hopes for the future. Similarly, Kendra G. laughed as she shared a story about starting a conversation with students about race in her art class that she couldn't turn off: "I just thought it was interesting, they didn't even want to do any art—they literally wanted to sit there and talk about race! And I'm like, 'OK guys, we gotta stop and this is great! We got to stop and we have to move into the lesson.'" Just as Beverly Tatum's writing reminded us in class, students began to see how the silence around talking about identity can be broken—and when it is, students (and educators) often relish the chance to share their ideas.

Art as a Tool

The most obvious takeaway for a group of arts educators is that many students realized that art can be a useful tool for talking about and connecting with people across different identities. Since many art teachers focus predominantly on technical instruction, the move to use art to teach about difference inspired several students. Often, as Jackie noted, in order to talk about topics as personal and fraught as who we are in relation to each other, we need some additional tools: "We need an object, like outside of ourselves—so that we can look at ourselves." Art can be that external object that helps us see ourselves differently. Jackie continued to explain why art can play this role: "It's not just history, it's not just a social movement, it's not just a picture of a person, it's something—art is what connects all of these fields. And it can connect so many different lines of work . . . coming together, reflecting the past, or thinking about the future. It all somehow comes together in art."

In her interview, Stefanie agreed, "Art is so subjective by nature and lends itself to conversations about perspective, culture, and identity. Making art or looking at art can connect and enhance understanding of another person's experience, or can help students be introspective about their own identities in new ways." Thinking about her own teaching experience, Stefanie shared an example of how art can build on these different interconnected elements to help us reveal new aspects of ourselves: "Sometimes . . . a student would be making a collage or painting, and we'd ask them to tell us about their work. As they described the piece and found the words to explain why a particular pattern or object represented them, they were able to unlock an undiscovered or new part of their identity they hadn't been able to articulate before making the art." Just as Stefanie's student was able to access a different part of his understanding, so too were students in the class. Art, as Avery reminded me, helps us "dig deeper" and to make the kinds of connections that help us better understand who we are and how we relate to the people around us.

STANCES IN THE K–12 CONTEXT

While much of this book focuses on working with preservice educators, many of the activities I facilitate for my own students could easily translate to younger audiences. According to many of my former students, they are already doing this in their own classrooms. Although a deeper analysis of how the stances might take shape in the K–12 context is necessary—perhaps in another book—the stories that many alumni of my course shared with me are useful testament to the potential for all educators to apply the stances in their work. Certainly, we could all—students and educators alike—benefit from practicing the stances that allow us to build relationships across difference. In the following section, I share several extended stories of useful strategies from former students—now teachers in their own classrooms—who have incorporated ideas from our work together as tools in their teaching.

GETTING STARTED

Emphasizing the need to get to know students, Rafael and Max each shared strategies that they employ in their classrooms to build trust and a sense of community.

Introductory Surveys

In Rafael's high school art class, he begins every year with an introductory survey to get to know his students as individuals. He said, "The survey starts off asking what their preferences are and aren't—what they like and what they don't like—and then it goes off into more personal cultural things. What's your favorite movie? What are your favorite foods? What's your favorite place to be? You end up learning a lot about their cultures just through those basic questions." These surveys offer Rafael an idea of how he might best relate to each student. Often, he smiles, it's through food. "I end up connecting a lot with my students through food because I like to eat a lot of food and so, when I have tried food from other cultures and they see that I know their food, it creates an instant connection with them, and then they're more interested in me for a minute." Once he finds that point of connection, Rafael has an opening: "Then I share a little bit of what I like, and from then on it's just a little bit easier to teach them for some reason—once we make that personal connection. Not an academic-based connection; it's more of a personal thing." The surveys also provide Rafael with crucial information to design his curriculum for the year in ways that respond to and expand upon students' own identities. He continued,

> Once I learn from those surveys where they're from and what they like, I try to choose artists and images from those respective countries or cultures. For example, I have a heavily Dominican and black population in my school, but I also have a small percentage of Mexicans and some [students] from Peru. If I know they are going to be in my class, I'll inject something in there from Peru, and then all of a sudden you see their eyes pop open, it's like "Oh my God! That's from my country, like I'm so glad." They never see it in the curriculum; they never see it anywhere else. Art happens to be one of those subjects where you can easily find art from any country or any culture and if you know your students then you can just easily plug it in anywhere. It takes a lot of planning ahead of time though.

When I asked Rafael why he continues this despite how time consuming it is, his reply underscored the importance of knowing one's students:

> One of the main things I learned is that a student is not going to want to learn from you unless they like you . . . And so you need to get to know your students first before you dive into your lesson plans—or before you dive into any lesson at all. [One must] humanize the teaching part by just getting to know them [the students] . . . it gives me a chance to not only hear what they like, but then at the end I also share what I like. So it's kind of like a back-and-forth—like just a human conversation about who we are, what we like and what we want to learn and what we don't like. Just that little bit

at the beginning sometimes is enough for that kid to be like, "Alright, I'm going to commit to you and listen in class and . . . not fool around so much."

Build Common Vocabulary

Working with a group of middle school students, Max expanded on the backpack-object activity we did in class to add a more focused discussion of stereotypes: "We took objects out of our bags as representations of ourselves, and then [students] used the objects as a metaphor for themselves. [We] asked how people perceived those objects and what they can assume about somebody or not assume about somebody and their identity." Max used the objects and the artwork they made of those objects as a starting point for introducing important terms such as stereotypes and assumptions: "We talked a lot about assumptions and stereotypes and just defining those and defining race. At one point [we] listed different stereotypes that people have about like Dominican people especially, because a lot of my students are Dominican. So we broke down what is a stereotype, what are stereotypes that we've been familiar with, and what is true, what is valid, what is completely false, or just inappropriate." As Max noted, this gave his class a chance to establish common vocabulary about challenging concepts and to talk about *how* to talk about identity.

NOTICING IN ACTION

Elle and Andy—both alumni of my course who are now full-time teachers—described recent lessons they had done with students that provided opportunities for them to notice what was important to their students. In constructing lessons with noticing in mind, they were able to pay close attention to the perspectives and ideas their students were sharing—ideas that those students rarely voiced aloud.

Neighborhood Art

Elle shared a lesson, similar to the community maps we created in class, that she was in the middle of with her elementary students that enabled her to learn more about their personal lives. Working with another teacher, they designed a lesson inspired by artist Romare Bearden's *The Block*. She said, "The students are making their own city blocks [depicting] their block where they live. Today, we were answering questions like 'What's the most important thing?' or 'Who were the most important people that you see in your day-to-day?' 'When you're walking from school back to home, what do you see? What do you feel? What do you hear?'" Elle and her co-teacher expanded on these questions to relate it to their artwork. "What colors represent them?" and "What represents their block?" As she listened to students and observed their artwork, she began to learn more about her students. "One student hears a lot of helicopters and car engine noises, and so he [creates] his apartment building and then a bodega on the corner and I think another building next to it, but then in front he did a collage of an exaggerated car—like the car is really big . . . and the helicopter and the sky [are] extra large to like emphasize those are the noises that he hears. One student is drawing [his block] from the perspective of his window, what he sees on his block." The project works because students are focusing on their own block, as Elle says, "they're not just choosing any ordinary New York City block, because there's a million of them, but they're choosing theirs and putting themselves into their block." As they do, they use tools of art—symbolism, scale, color—so "it's not a direct recreation of a photograph of what it is . . . so it's a way for them to express their identity that they feel connected to their home which is automatically a part of their identity." The students' works of art help Elle notice what is important to them:

> It's helpful to learn what's important to them and what they're noticing about where they live. It's back to that human connection of developing a relationship and understanding where they're coming from. This is good because it's their home . . . we're talking about their homes, and that can sometimes be a private thing or something that maybe they don't bring to school, they kind of leave that at the door. Then I'm this adult that they don't necessarily know, so they're able to talk about things and maybe things that they notice and see are uncomfortable. One of the students is definitely like, "Miss, I don't want to draw this because my neighborhood is just full of crack heads in the projects. Why would I want to make that?" The fact that they are able to, they feel comfortable telling me those things, that opens up a conversation. Then I can be like "Ok, well what would be your dream location of a block if you don't feel comfortable doing where you live?" Or "What would you change about it? How can you illustrate that change?" I guess what I'm talking about is that they're creating something and we can build a relationship through discussing, in his case what he would change about it . . . we're just getting to know each other better.

Self-Portraits

Similar to Elle's description of the neighborhood artworks that students made, Andy shared how a lesson on self-portraits can help him practice noticing what his high school students value. In prefacing his description of this project, Andy noted how he intentionally tries to slow down to bring "patience, awareness, and open-mindedness" to his teaching. We were talking in his classroom, so Andy points to a specific image on the wall: "The one—the middle row all the way to the right with the blue background. That student had—we had a good relationship—but he had a lot of bravado about how successful he considered himself in this school . . . if I pushed him [with constructive feedback], he would get mad at me. But then he made this self-portrait and what he has around his neck is a necklace with a report card with all of these failing grades on it. And it's about this past about having failed seventh grade or something like that." Suddenly Andy realized there was more to his student's bravado than he had first assumed: "You know, if I had said put your most like embarrassing part of your past somehow into the image, he would have been like 'heck no.' But they did an exercise before making the self-portrait that was [focused on] what's an important object to you? What's a formative experience? And they did some sketching. And then [the prompt] was 'How could you work one or two of these things into your self-portrait?'" Looking at the work together, Andy described how the student's choice to share this personal information was "really intense" and, in noticing it, Andy came to better understand his student and their relationship. Reflecting on his teaching, Andy noted that projects such as the self-portraits enable him to "take the moments of noticing what a student is offering or seeing an in and not just going full-speed ahead with my structure or my agenda, or what I'm hoping they'll get done . . . to be ready to hear them kind of open a door and not blow past it because you're in a school and because there's learning targets they're supposed to meet and because they were late and because of all the things that can be—because of the institution—hard to keep at bay. To keep that space."

WONDERING IN ACTION

Reminiscing about lessons they had each recently taught, former students Jasmin and Jane each advocated for open-ended inquiry questions as a key strategy to spark a sense of wondering among their students. Through strategically crafted questions, they have been able to move students into critical analyses of power and privilege through discussions about works of art.

Guided Inquiry Discussion

While telling about a lesson she had recently taught her high school students on the Ghanaian-born artist El Anatsui, Jane highlighted how she used specific guided questions to spark a wondering stance in her class: "Today we were looking at [a work of art by] El Anatsui and we were talking about why the Metropolitan Museum of Art chose to put it in the African gallery versus in the contemporary [gallery]." To encourage her students to critically interrogate the systems that dictate how our identities are prioritized by external forces, she led with the question, "Why was that decision made?" Jane went on to describe how this question prompted a lively debate about how the museum had chosen to use El Anatsui's nationality as his primary identifier over the fact that he is currently making artwork. This kind of critical discussion opened up multiple points for analyzing the nature of identity, privilege, and power. Jane's anecdote also points to another kind of inquiry when she ruminates on her own use of questioning to wonder about her identity: "In teaching . . . about works of art and asking questions of other people and helping them to think about it . . . asking those questions and analyzing the world, that's helped me to sort of form my identity." Here Jane suggests that her role as a teacher is to encourage her students to question and analyze the world. Yet, there's more: Jane finds that when she cultivates chances for her students to question and wonder, she too uses those opportunities to reflect on her own identity.

Similarly, Jasmin described a lesson she taught in her high school classroom that relied on a set of inquiry questions to encourage wondering by her students: "At night school, we were looking at Edward Hopper's *Neighborhood* paintings, and just by me telling the students that they were called neighborhood paintings, they all automatically were like, 'Well that's not what my neighborhood looks like.' So, that started a whole other conversation with [the prompt], 'What's similar about your neighborhood and Hopper's? What's different? Why do you think this is that? . . . Or can you tell what's his ethnic background or what neighborhood is he from based on his paintings? Do you know other places that seem like this?'" Jasmin noted that this approach of continually peppering her lessons with open-ended questions has led to animated and critical conversations throughout her teaching.

RESEARCHING IN ACTION

As seasoned educators, Jasmin and Rafael shared several lessons as we talked about their approaches to helping students do research to contextualize their understanding of identity. Through making contextually specific connections and creating counternarratives, students learned to see the interrelatedness of different identities.

Local Connections

For a recent lesson focused on graffiti, Rafael started with a comprehensive historical overview of graffiti throughout different time periods and cultures: "I show them videos and clips of where graffiti started—how there was graffiti in Rome, and in the thirties, the hobos used to use it. But then there was a really big boom in the sixties in Philadelphia and New York, and then I'll show them videos of what the trains looked like." Building on this history, Rafael switched to a more local perspective: "Then I go into different graffiti artists from the Bronx, specifically from the Bronx [where his school is located], and then they get really excited: 'Oh I've seen this guy's stuff already!'" From there, Rafael designed a field trip to explore their school neighborhood. "And then we'll go on a walk and then show them, 'Oh this is Tat's Crew [a New York City–based graffiti collective]. Look at this wall across the street, these guys are Tat's Crew too.'" This kind of locally based teaching roots students in their own unique context—a move that helps them see their environment through a different lens. Rafael continued, "For example, if I'm teaching them bubble lettering, I can take a walk around the immediate school and there's some of the best graffiti artists in the South Bronx—it's right there." Often, Rafael has invited guest artists to his classroom to further this local learning; students have a chance to meet artists from their own neighborhood and to make connections between the artwork they see and their own life experiences. By teaching his students to see the interconnected context of the world around them, to look for artwork in their own local spaces, their relationships to their neighborhoods change. They become more active observers of their own streets and, better yet, see the artwork within their own spaces.

Remixed Stories

In her lesson entitled, "Fairy Tales: The Remix," Jasmin asks her students to rewrite fairy tales to offer a new perspective on the original story: "We read classic fairy tales by the Brothers Grimm. We talk about plot, settings, social context, etc. . . . Then we just totally flip it and remix it into something else. We change the plot. We change the setting. We change the ethnicity of the characters. We change everything about the story. And then at the end, [students] have to explain why they felt it needed it." When I asked Jasmin about her goals for the lesson, she spoke about the importance of allowing students to analyze and rewrite the narratives they are taught by society. "Rapunzel should be Jamaican and have long dreads, instead of blonde and European, right?" she said. Jasmin continued to reflect on her teaching decisions: "I wanted to give them the power. I want them to have complete choice and complete empowerment over how things turn out. [I tell them], 'If you are not in the happily-ever-after kind of mood, you don't have to be, right?' 'If you feel like a brunette should be the prettiest and fairest of them all, go for it! . . . If you feel like you have to rewrite a story to make that moral or that lesson apparent, then do so.' 'Cause there's obviously some disparities going on in the world. People are still stereotyping."

As her students create their reimagined fairly tales—tales that reinvent characters as different gender, racial, or ethnic identities—they critique the ways they have been taught to see themselves and each other. Jasmin describes how she wants to empower her students to see themselves as agents; she wants them to think, "'That's my piece of power. That I know that the person who originally wrote this story meant for her to have skin as white as snow, rose-red lips, straight shiny black raven hair. That even though that's what they wanted to do, that I have the power to do this. Just one little simple tool like a crayon; I just changed someone's whole entire opinion or viewpoint and made it my own.'" She continued, "This is my little piece of trying to make [the disparities and stereotyping] stop, or like at least, showing [students] that it's possible. Like, maybe just this one class is not going to change their whole entire outlook on like race or religion or gender or sexual orientation, but it's like a start to make other people aware like it's possible."

CONNECTING IN ACTION

Because murals have a long history of serving as tools for sharing and co-creating, it is not surprising that both Jennifer and Rafael facilitated collaborative mural projects with their students. Easily adapted for any age group, collaborative murals provide opportunities for participants to exchange ideas, co-construct images together, and build connections with each other in the process.

Collaborative Murals

Rafael told about a mural he made with his high school art class, including a group who had just arrived in New York City from Yemen:

> It was right when those kids came in from Yemen and one of them I remember, his name is Muhammed—very sweet kid, very respectful. We were doing a mural that says "love" and "life" and in the center there was a big lotus flower to represent life and rebirth. We were looking at it and Muhammed was there—he was helping us and I just had the idea . . . I was like, "Muhammed, how do you write love and life in Arabic?" and he showed me. I was like, "You want to do it on the wall?" and he was like, "Sure!" and so he drew it for me and then I did a stencil for him and put it up. Now, when all the other Yemeni kids came by and they saw that, they were like, "Oh wow! They actually put Arabic writing on the school wall!" Like, they felt a little bit more accepted and more comfortable around their surroundings after that because it did come during a tense time—they came from straight-up war. And then finally to be in somewhere where they don't have to see dead bodies or hear bombs going off. And you can see the difference between how they view the world and how my students who live here view the world. It's very different.

Rafael described a follow-up poetry event at the school where Muhammed shared a poem about his experiences in Yemen: "To hear his experience, it was just one poem that one time and everybody was just in silence listening to him. And so I think after that day everybody was a lot more accepting and it was pretty cool to see how the whole school kind of embraced these new students that came in, especially after that poem." While simply inviting Muhammed to add an Arabic word to a mural and to share a poem may seem inconsequential, such tiny actions can have large consequences. By recognizing and honoring Muhammed's multiple identities (Arabic speaker, immigrant, new student, poet), Rafael and his colleagues opened an opportunity for him to share those identities with the entire school community. In doing so, the walls between the new Yemeni students and the existing student body began to crumble. As Rafael's story illustrates, part of this work requires educators and students alike to challenge the conventional view of the teacher as the sole purveyor of knowledge and students as recipients. As Muhammed taught Rafael and his classmates Arabic words and recited a poem from his own experience, he became the teacher.

Working in an elementary school, Jennifer described another collaborative mural project that she was in the middle of facilitating in partnership with the nearby middle school and an outside community mural organization: "The theme of the mural is about the diversity of Ridgewood and about respect for the different communities and the different cultural backgrounds. It's been a way to engage the kids on those topics, to create symbols that may represent diversity, respect, the different cultures." Jennifer noted that she's already witnessing different kinds of conversations: "With the younger students who haven't thought that much about these topics yet . . . the mural has been a good way to start that conversation." Jennifer described the questions about students' individual cultures, such as "talking about what kinds of foods do you eat in your family? Or what kinds of celebrations do you have? Or talking about the families' stories of immigration and how they might be similar or different from other people's families?" have led to "discussions in groups about immigration history, about food celebrations, culture." Reflecting on what she's learned, she's observed that "by having those conversations with each other, they've realized similarities and differences—that the cultures are distinct from each other . . . I think that even for me it was surprising to hear how different the experience can be for the kids and how much of the culture—and almost all the students are immigrants or their parents are—is retained in the house. I didn't realize how traditional the cuisine was [for] most of them . . . so there was that exchange with each other . . . in a consciousness-raising way." This exchange of ideas is particularly important right now. As Jennifer shared her hopes for the mural, she pointed to the current political climate: "I know that in this political climate, a lot of the students have said that they feel afraid or disrespected, [they are] feeling kind of low about their own background and about how others feel towards them. So I was also hoping that we could reflect a different vision of cultures living harmoniously. I'm hoping we'll build that with the students. So for anyone who works there or anyone who comes into the building, it can be a banner that we wave. This is who we are, we're proud."

The anecdotes of these stances in action highlight how educators can transform and adapt activities in this book to meet the needs and align with the strengths of their own teaching contexts. Certainly, there is no standard curriculum for this kind of work. By its very nature, it must be rooted in the contexts in which learners and educators meet each other. It must be flexible, responsive, improvisational, and ever evolving. Yet, efforts to pay attention to the stances in all of our teaching—from the ways we think about planning to the kinds of assignments we design, the sources we introduce, the questions we ask, and the ways we create and share work—can help us move toward a kind of teaching that seeks to build stronger relationships across our different identities. As Kendra G., an elementary school teacher and former student in my class, noted, when we shift our teaching to really get to know the lives of our students, to see and hear them for who they are in this world, we empower them to carry forth a similar sense of connection, empathy, and understanding into their own lives:

> I think for this generation, or generations to come, it helps them to be able to have their own agency and to be able to speak up for themselves. If we can do that for them as art teachers, or as teachers in general, it would only benefit them in their future. To have a real self-awareness and an understanding of who they are as they go out into the world, because if they don't have that, it's going to be even harder . . . They have—just like we have lives outside of work—there's so much that they value that it's important for us to bring it into education. I don't think we do enough of it. I just think we have to figure out how to do more of it."

"GETTING TO KNOW YOU" AND "YOU'VE GOT TO BE CAREFULLY TAUGHT"

My grandmother loved musicals. When I stayed with her, she would often sing to me from the Rodgers and Hammerstein musicals *The King and I* and *South Pacific.*[2] Although these musicals contain deeply damaging stereotypes, the stories they tell have also prompted national conversations about identity both at the time of their original release and upon each subsequent theatrical reprise. Today, as I consider the role of art in teaching and learning about identity, two songs stick in my mind as I teach. The first one, "Getting to Know You," is sung by the teacher in *The King and I*. She sings about the need to get to know each of her students, offering important advice for educators: "If you become a teacher/ by your pupils you'll be taught." Or, as Rafael adamantly proclaimed: "It is a *must* to get to know your students' backgrounds and interests!" Good teaching enables students to teach the teacher as we get to know them as complex people.

As simple as this concept sounds—particularly when sung to a catchy melody—it is remarkably complicated for many educators. If the number of books and articles on the subject is any measure, it appears that getting to know our students is so challenging that we often ignore it and rarely master it. Calling for a move to "reality pedagogy," educator-scholar Christopher Emdin advises educators to move out of the physical boundaries and psychological limitations of their classrooms to get to know the realities of their students' lives.[3] His suggestions for helping teachers get to know the lives of their students echo the work of progressive educator-scholars such as Rich Milner, Dorinda Carter Andrews, Lisa Delpit, Sonia Nieto, Leigh Patel, bell hooks, Bill Ayers, and Mica Pollock. These educators point to the need for building bridges that connect the lives of educators with the lives of students in order to meet the logistical challenges of classroom organization and the pedagogical concerns of liberatory education.

The second song that has wriggled its way from my grandmother's mouth into my head comes from *South Pacific*. Crooning to his children about racial prejudice, the character Lieutenant Cable explains how the walls that exist between people are built intentionally: "You've got to be taught/ To hate and fear, you've got to be taught/ from year to year/ It's got to be drummed in your dear little ear/ You've got to be carefully taught." While "Getting to Know You" speaks of bridges, "You've Got to Be Carefully Taught" reminds us of the borders we knowingly build between us. To speak solely of education as the perfect tool for developing understanding risks hiding how it has long been a tool for perpetuating prejudice. Even the most well-intentioned educator arrives at her work with assumptions about her own identity, the identities of her students, and the ways in which those may or may not align. The social messages, cues, codes, and policies that make up our worlds clearly delineate the borders between differing groups of people— often to the benefit of specific groups. In other words, from the moment we begin the work of teaching, the lines have already been drawn. Or, as Rodgers and Hammerstein point out, we have already been carefully taught who is one of us, and who is not.

How are we to merge the lessons of these two songs? Certainly, we must get to know our students for who they are as individuals and members of a collective society. And, just as we seek to know our students, we must also seek to know ourselves—to learn to see how we have each been carefully taught to believe in the barriers between us. These conversations are hard—they are emotional, provocative, and jarring at times. But they could not be more necessary. To ignore teaching and learning about identity is to stand on the side of the status quo and to declare through our inaction that it doesn't matter. Nothing could be further from the truth; who we are matters.

As Jasmin, a veteran classroom teacher, noted, "[I]f you're gonna be in education, there's not gonna be anytime ever where you will not have to interact with a room full of people who you may or may not be able to relate to, and who may or may not be able to relate to each other because of certain themes or stereotypes, because of identity." The only way we can navigate the complexity of identity is to take it head on: we must learn to name, analyze, reimagine, critique, and reflect on how our identities influence our experiences in the world. You cannot do this without talking candidly, authentically, and with care about identity. In other words, good teaching requires us to engage with the complexity of identity. It may not be as simple as humming a Broadway tune, but with a concerted effort, it might not actually be as hard as we think.

Suggested Artists

There is no way that I could include a complete—or even simply compre-hensive—list of artists whose work can be used to teach about who we are in relation to each other; nearly every artist somehow conveys important ideas about what it means to be human. This list is merely a starting point for additional research. I compiled it from artists whose work I have shared in my courses and from the collected research that students have shared in our conversations (conversations which take place in New York City, in the United States, and at a particular moment in time that certainly shapes this list). In putting together this starter list—and I underscore that it is only a starter list—I have included some very general keywords to describe the media within which the artist works, some description of the aesthetics of their work, and some topical issues they address in their work. These key-words are by no means exhaustive. For each artist, I have included a web-site where you can find additional information and images (available at the time of publication). While many of the artists referenced here regularly exhibit their work in public venues, *every* community has local artists who may or may not have the same visibility as the artists listed here; seek out these local artists through research into community arts organizations, as they can offer uniquely local perspectives.

Belkis Ayón: Printmaking; Cuba, collagraphy; process-based, allegorical, Afro Cuban mythology; Abakuá society, silhouettes, imposed silence. http://www.elmuseo.org/nkame-belkis-ayon/

Firelei Báez: Works on paper, Dominican Republic, anthropology, science fiction, black female subjectivity, women's work, humor, fantasy, diasporic society, cultural ambiguities, metaphysical, cultural invasion.
http://fireleibaez.com

Francisca Benitez: Performance, dance, drawing, Chile, boundaries, architecture, sign language, gesture, communication.
http://www.Franciscabenitez.org

Dawoud Bey: Photographer, portraiture, everyday life, marginalized people, African American life, documentary, Harlem.
http://stephendaitergallery.com/artists/dawoud-bey/

Jordan Casteel: Painter, snapshot, everyday life, portraiture, black life, black masculinity, social justice.
http://www.jordancasteel.com

Kiran Chandra: Drawing, installation, India, language, systems, the natural world, cultural connections.
http://kiran-chandra-hssx.squarespace.com/about-avenue/

Renee Cox: Photography, self-portraiture, Jamaica, black womanhood, black female sexuality, religious imagery, black representation, the nude.
http://www.reneecox.org

Aisha Cousins: Performance, art scores, narratives, interactive, live, contrasting history, shared sociological shifts, black identity.
http://www.aishacousins.com

Damaris Cruz: Photography, mural, community, public art, street art, everyday life, celebratory, Puerto Rican life and culture.
https://dlola.tumblr.com

Priyanka Dasgupta: Video, sound, research, lineage, immigration, photography, India, diaspora.
http://priyankadasgupta.com

Abigail Deville: Immersive installation, site-specific, marginalized people and places, found objects, forgotten stories, trash, treasure.
https://art21.org/artist/abigail-deville/

John Edmonds: Photography, documentary, fashion, black masculinity, gay masculinity, fashion, portraiture, marginalized people, intimacy, black male identity, performativity, third consciousness.
http://www.johnedmondsphoto.com

Rachel Farmer: Ceramics, sculpture, quilting, westward expansion, feminism, pioneers, queer identity, Mormon faith, ancestry, stories of survival, community.
http://rachelfarmer.com

Ana Teresa Fernández: Social sculptures, performance, gendered-labor, immigration, class, sex, American Mexican border.
http://anateresafernandez.com/

Samuel Fosso: Studio photography, identity, gender, Nigeria, Central African Republic, pattern, dress, Black cultural movements, disguise.
https://www.icp.org/browse/archive/constituents/samuel-fosso?all/all/all/all/0

LaToya Ruby Frazier: Photography, video, performance, marginalized people, documentary, industrialism, Rust Belt revitalization, environmental justice, health-care inequity, family, communal history.
http://www.latoyarubyfrazier.com

Genevieve Gaignard: Photographer, sculpture, installation, self-portraiture, dual identity, race, gender, intersectionality, feminine ritual, performativity, humor, persona.
http://www.genevievegaignard.com/home

Carmen Lomas Garza: Painting, Chicano movement, family, domestic scenes, everyday life, activism, positive depictions, narrative, personal history.
http://carmenlomasgarza.com/

Heather Hart: Multimedia, installation, futurism, distorted tradition, viewer activation, participation, liminal space, questioning, creating alternative narratives.
https://www.heather-hart.com

Sukjong Hong: Comic/graphic journalism, labor violations, labor, activism, architecture, urban planning, humanism, Asian American community, housing, militarism.
http://sukjonghong.com

Erin Ikeler: Painter, text-based, language, queer identity, naming, legibility, signs, puns, allusion, language and gay culture, gay history, feminism.
http://eeikeler.com/about

JR: Photography, global, portraiture, street artist, public art, collaborative, community, social action.
http://www.jr-art.net

Brian Jungen: Mixed media, installation, disassemblage, Dunne-Za heritage, consumer goods, transforming material, process-based, masks.
https://art21.org/artist/brian-jungen/

Christine Sun Kim: Sound artist, performance, the deaf experience, sign language, subtitles, written conversation, email, text messages, technology, language, nonverbal communication, filtered reality, distortion, translation, unlearning societal etiquette.
http://www.christinesunkim.com

Deana Lawson: Photography, the body, social histories, familial legacy, community, romance, religious and spiritual aesthetics, figurative, documentary, family, domestic environments, blackness.
http://www.sikkemajenkinsco.com/index.php?v=artist&artist=580a604ccbdfa

Nikki S. Lee: Photography, performance, subcultures, fluidity, race, class, fashion, assimilation, Korea.
http://www.tonkonow.com/lee.html

Shaun Leonardo: Performance, drawing, masculinity, policing, the body, sport, participatory art.
http://elcleonardo.com/statement

Glenn Ligon: Interdisciplinary, cultural identity, social identity, found sources, Afro-centric, civil rights, American identity, sexual politics, slavery, literature, blackness, text-based.
http://www.glennligonstudio.com

Amos Mac: Photography, publisher, queer culture, gender fluidity, portraiture, storytelling, vulnerability, intimacy, trans representation.
https://www.amosmac.com

Ana Mendieta: Photography, sculpture, Cuba, film, earth-body, performance, gender bending, fluidity, immigration, exiled, displacement.
http://www.alisonjacquesgallery.com/artists/47-ana-mendieta/works/

Wangechi Mutu: Collage, painting, feminism, Kenya, the female body, found materials, cultural identity, colonial history, fashion, contemporary African politics, sexual repression, anthropology, masks, migration, magazine cutouts, racial distortion, traditional African crafts, storytelling, myth making, endangered cultural heritage.
http://wangechimutu.com/art/

Hương Ngô: performance, installation, immigration, Vietnam, political history, language, American South, surveillance, anti-colonialism, women in activism, power.
http://www.huongngo.com

Chris Ofili: Interdisciplinary, blaxploitation films, modernist painting, blackness, representation, dual spirituality, mystical, kaleidoscopic paintings, Trinidad and Tobago, United Kingdom, abstract figuration, glitter, collage, Zimbabwean cave paintings, intersectionality.
https://www.davidzwirner.com/artists/chris-ofili

Catherine Opie: Photography, lesbian culture, lesbian identity, gender, fluidity, queerness, portraiture, landscape, feminism, gender performativity.
https://art21.org/artist/catherine-opie/

Sondra Perry: Media artist, video, installation, digital technology, systemic oppression, black identity, intersectionality, blackness, technology, image production, image culture, duality, intelligence, seductivity, black family heritage, black history, black femininity.
http://sondraperry.com/

Gordon Parks: Photographer, documentary, social justice, midcentury American culture, race relations, poverty, civil rights, urban life.
http://www.gordonparksfoundation.org

Shani Peters: Community building, activism, politics, power, youth, black identity, mixed media, participatory art.
http://www.shanipeters.com

Adrian Piper: Interdisciplinary, nontraditional media, photo-text collage, drawing, video installation, performance, sound works, concrete specificity, object of awareness, conceptual, agency, individual identity, metaphysical, political, race, gender, social contract reform, philosophy, political reconstruction.
http://www.adrianpiper.com

Annie Pootoogook: Drawing, contemporary Inuit life and experience, women in northern Canada, northern Canadian life, everyday life, hardships of northern Canadian communities, impact of technology on Inuit life, home, interior scenes, alcoholism, violence, domestic abuse.
http://feheleyfinearts.com/artists/annie-pootoogook/

Christina Quarles: painter, figurative, queer identity, mixed identity, mistaken identity, multiplicity, ambiguity, abstraction, black ancestry, categorical identity.
http://www.christinaquarles.com

Wendy Red Star: Photography, sculpture, video, fiber arts, and performance, Native American ideologies, colonialist structures, self-portraiture.
http://www.wendyredstar.com

Faith Ringgold: Painter, interdisciplinary, feminist, African American experience, folk art, equality, activism, institutional critique.

http://www.faithringgold.com

Julio Salgado: Graphic arts, immigrant experience, deportation, dreamers, politics, refugee, identity through activism, social reform, do-it-yourself, social media.
http://juliosalgadoart.com

Tamara Santibañez: Painter, tattoo artist, interdisciplinary artist, publisher, religious symbolism, punk, subcultural semiotics, fetish, Chicanx art, cultural signifiers, coded communication, marginalized people, iconography.
http://tamarasantibanez.com

Judith Scott: Sculpture, form, cocoons, the body, found material, yarn, pairs, totemic poles.
http://judithandjoycescott.com

Tschabalala Self: Painter, emotional, physical, psychological, the black female body, intersectionality, race, gender, sexuality, black femininity, self-realization, multiplicity.
http://tschabalalaself.com

Sarah Sense: Mixed media, Native American, collage, photography, printmaking, Chitimacha, tradition, ancestral designs, tribal patterns, basketweaving, storytelling.
www.sarahsense.com

Cindy Sherman: Photography, performance, self-portraiture, vulnerability, power, identity, perceptions of self, feminism.
https://www.moma.org/interactives/exhibitions/2012/cindysherman/

Shahzia Sikander: Miniature painting, Pakistan, installation, animation, formal tropes, contested cultural and political history, process-based, miniature tradition.
http://www.shahziasikander.com

Lorna Simpson: Photography, multimedia, race, gender, African American experience/identity, conceptual, text and image, discrimination, violence, feminism, hair.

http://www.lsimpsonstudio.com

Martine Syms: Interdisciplinary, video, text-based, technology, blackness, Afrofuturism, black lesbians culture/history, conceptual, entrepreneur, publishing, queer theory, power, language, spirituality.
http://martinesyms.com

Mickalene Thomas: Photography, paintings, rhinestones, elaborate, portraiture, beauty, blackness, female identity, pop culture, sexuality, race, gender, power.
http://mickalenethomas.com/

Kara Walker: Painter, interdisciplinary, blackness, civil war, race, gender, sexuality, black history, slavery, figurative, theatrical, silhouettes, violence, paper, cutouts, Victorian.
http://sikkemajenkinsco.com/index.php?v=artist&artist=4eece69f3eb4e

Carrie Mae Weems: Photography, verse, performance, African American history, race, class, gender identity, family, gender roles, motherhood, activism.
http://carriemaeweems.net/

Ai Weiwei: Interdisciplinary, protest, dissent, bureaucratic power structures, criticism, mass consumption, migration.
http://aiweiwei.com

Kehinde Wiley: Painter, glorification, black representation, figurative, history, prestige, black male masculinity, floral, juxtaposition, interrupting tropes.
http://kehindewiley.com

Didier William: Printmaking, Haiti, painter, deconstructed bodies, abstraction, figurative, fragmented bodies, reassemblage, figurative identities, secondary body, secondary identity, material figuration.
http://www.didierwilliam.com

Fred Wilson: Museums, critique, public art, racism, power, memory, sculpture, monuments, black identity.

https://www.pacegallery.com/artists/507/fred-wilson

David Wojnarowicz: Painter, photography, performance, activism, gay identity, AIDs activism, civil rights, pop culture.
http://www.artnet.com/artists/david-wojnarowicz/

Sasha Wortzel: Film, documentary, queer identity, transgender identity, America, relationships, nature, ignored histories.
http://www.sashawortzel.com

Suggested Readings

Thoughtful resources about identity awareness, community building, cultural relevancy, social justice education, and cross-identity relationship building can offer educators both theoretical lenses and practical strategies for teaching. For purposes of brevity, I've selected some of the typical readings I assign in my course "Identity, Community, and Culture in Art Education." These are organized according to the units I teach within the course in the order I introduce them.

RECOGNIZING OUR OWN LAYERED IDENTITIES

Why does who we are matter in education?

Beverly Tatum, *Why Are All the Black Kids Sitting Together in the Cafeteria* (New York: Basic Books).

Ana María Villegas and Tamara Lucas, "Preparing Culturally Responsive Teachers: Rethinking the Curriculum," *Journal of Teacher Education* 53, no. 1 (2002): 20–32, doi: 10.1177/0022487102053001003.

William Ayers, Maxine Greene, and Ryan Alexander-Tanner, introduction, *Art and Social Justice Education: Culture as Commons*, by Therese Quinn et al. (New York: Routledge, 2012), xi–xvi.

Dipti Desai and Graeme Chalmers, "Notes for a Dialogue on Art Education in Critical Times," *Art Education* 60, no. 5 (2007): 6–12.

RELATING ACROSS SOCIAL DIVISIONS

How do our multiple identities shape our views of the world and our students? How can we make sense of who we are as it relates to our work as educators? What reflection tools can we use to unpack the significance of our own stories and community connections?

Lucy R. Lippard, "Around Here," in *The Lure of the Local: Senses of Place in a Multicentered Society* (New York: New Press, 1997).

Kimberly Powell, "Viewing Places: Students as Visual Ethnographers," *Art Education* 63, no. 6 (2010): 44.

Özlem Sensoy and Robin DiAngelo, *Is Everyone Really Equal?* (New York: Teacher's College Press, 2011).

Audre Lorde, "A Litany for Survival," in *The Black Unicorn* (New York: Norton Publishing, 1978), 31.

Claudia Rankine, (2014) "Citizen," *Poetry Magazine*, March 2014, https://www.poetryfoundation.org/poetrymagazine/poems/detail/56848.

IDENTITY, POWER, AND TEACHING

What biases, expectations, and assumptions do we carry with us? How do we navigate those with our students? What role does power play in our relationships with students and communities? What reflection tools can we use to unpack the significance of our own stories and community connections?

Lisa Delpit, *Other People's Children: Cultural Conflict in the Classroom* (New York: New Press, 2006).

"Teaching 'Black Lives Matter' SLJ Talks to Educator, Author Renée Watson," *School Library Journal*, December 2014, http://www.slj.com/2014/12/diversity/teaching-black-lives-matter-slj-talks-to-educator-author-renee-watson/.

Leisy Wyman and Grant Kashatok, "Getting to Know Students' Communities," in *Everyday Antiracism: Getting Real About Race in School*, ed. Mica Pollock et al. (New York: New Press, 2008), 299–304.

Joshua Aronson, "Knowing Students as Individuals," in *Everyday Antiracism: Getting Real About Race in School*, ed. Mica Pollock (New York: New Press, 2008).

Kristina Rizga, "What White teachers Can Learn from Black Preachers," *Mother Jones*, April 26, 2016, http://www.motherjones.com/politics/2016/04/white-teachers-black-students-discipline-education-emdin/.

STRATEGIES FOR TEACHING ABOUT IDENTITY

What are effective approaches to teaching identity in art education? How can we create learning experiences that help us unpack the complexity of identity?

Dipti Desai, Jessica Hamlin, and Rachel Mattson, *Constructing Race. History as Art, Art as History* (New York: Routledge, 2010), 147–95.

Sheng Kuan Chung, "Media Literacy Art Education: Deconstructing Lesbian and Gay Stereotypes in the Media," *International Journal of Art & Design Education* 26, no. 1 (2007): 98–107, doi: 10.1111/j.1476-8070.2007.00514.x.

Karen Keifer-Boyd, Patricia M. Amburgy, and Wanda B. Knight, "Unpacking Privilege: Memory, Culture, Gender, Race, and Power in Visual Culture," *Art Education* 60, no. 3 (2007): 19.

Joshua Aronson, "Knowing Students as Individuals," in *Everyday Antiracism: Getting Real About Race in School*, ed. Mica Pollock (New York: New Press, 2008), 67–69.

Alexandra Lightfoot, "Using Photography to Explore Racial Identity," in *Everyday Antiracism: Getting Real About Race in School*, ed. Mica Pollock et al. (New York: New Press, 2008), 142–45.

Rita Tenorio, "Brown Kids Can't Be in Our Club," in *Rethinking Multicultural Education*, ed. Wayne Au (Milwaukee, WI: Rethinking Schools, 2014).

Alejandro Segura-Mora, "What Color Is Beautiful?," in *Rethinking Multicultural Education*, ed. Wayne Au (Milwaukee, WI: Rethinking Schools, 2014).

Linda Christensen, "For My People," in *Rethinking Multicultural Education*, ed. Wayne Au (Milwaukee, WI: Rethinking Schools, 2014).

CULTURE AND COMMUNITY

What do we mean by culture? How can we learn about the complexity of a culture in order to teach about it? How can we teach in ways that are culturally relevant and affirming of our students?

Lucy R. Lippard, *Mixed Blessings: New Art in a Multicultural America* (New York: Pantheon Books, 1990), 1–18.

Ulyssa Martinez, "Cultura(ally) Jammed: Culture Jams as a Form of Culturally Relevant Teaching," *Art Education* 65, no. 5, (2012): 12–17.

"Danger of a Single Story," YouTube: TED Talk, https://www.youtube.com/watch?v=D9Ihs241zeg&index=4&list=PLrMqXQ2J_13ubw2OiTy9Fd kAYHm_y2IIy.

Alice Lai, "Culturally Responsive Art Education in a Global Era," *Art Education* 65, no. 5 (2012): 18–23.

STRATEGIES FOR TEACHING ABOUT CULTURE

What strategies do museum or arts educators use to teach about art from multiple cultural perspectives? What are common pitfalls in teaching about culture in the arts? How can we delve deeply into works of art to learn about how culture shapes people's experiences?

Elizabeth Schlessman, "Aquí y Allá," in *Rethinking Multicultural Education*, ed. Wayne Au (Milwaukee, WI: Rethinking Schools, 2014).

Steven Picht-Trujillo and Paola Suchsland, "Putting a Human Face on the Immigration Debate," in *Rethinking Multicultural Education*, ed. Wayne Au (Milwaukee, WI: Rethinking Schools, 2014).

William Ayers, *To Teach: The Journey of a Teacher* (New York: Teachers College Press, 2001), 67–80.

Christine Ballengee-Morris and Pamela Taylor, "You Can Hide but You Can't Run: Interdisciplinary and Culturally Sensitive Approaches to Mask Making," *Art Education* 58, no. 5 (2005): 12–17.

Judith Dobrynski, "Honoring Art, Honoring Artists," *New York Times*, February 3, 2011, http://www.nytimes.com/2011/02/06/arts/design/06names.html?_r=1.

Barbara Kirshenblatt-Gimblett, "An Accessible Aesthetic: The Role of Folk Arts and the Folk Artist in the Curriculum," *New York Folklore: The Journal of the New York Folklore Society* 9, no. 3-4 (1983): 9–18.

Lucy R. Lippard, *Mixed Blessings: New Art in a Multicultural America* (New York: Pantheon Books, 1990).

ART, AGENCY, AND POWER

How can we use the arts to upend ideological inequality? What role does teaching play in the quest for a more just society? How can art be a tool to have an impact on conditions of injustice in our communities? Why can art be used to engage communities? What are the challenges and opportunities of community-based art?

Paulo Freire, *Pedagogy of the Oppressed* (New York: Continuum Press, 1970).

Shannon Brinkley, "Learning to Lead: Lessons from a Farm Village," *Art Education* 68, no. 4 (2015): 7–13.

Keith Knight and Mat Schwarzman, *Beginner's Guide to Community-Based Arts* (Oakland, CA: New Village Press. 2005).

Korina Jocson and Brett Cook, "Pedagogy, Collaboration, and Transformation: A conversation with Brett Cook," in *Art and Social Justice Education: Culture as Commons*, ed. Therese M. Quinn et al. (New York: Routledge, 2012) 89–94.

Paul Kuttner, "What is Cultural Organizing?," *Cultural Organizing* (blog), 2015, http://culturalorganizing.org/what-is-cultural-organizing/.

"A Simple Mouse Can Get You," *CultureStrike*, http://culturestrike.tumblr.com/tagged/culturestrike-magazine.

"How We Work," *CultureStrike*, http://www.culturestrike.org/how-we-work.

ART-MAKING RESOURCES

There are many excellent tutorials online for making zines, comics, and initiating collaborative art projects. In addition, here are a few suggested resources to launch additional research.

Zines

Arzu Mistry and Todd Elkin, *The Accordion Book Project*, https://accordionbook-project.com.

Booklyn Education Manual, https://booklyn.org/category/education/.

Comics

Scott McCloud, *Understanding Comics: the Invisible Art* (New York: HarperPerennial, 1994).

Lynda Barry, *Syllabus: Notes from an Accidental Professor* (Montreal: Drawn & Quarterly, 2015).

Jessica Abel and Matt Madden, *Drawing Words & Writing Pictures: Making Comics: Manga, Graphic Novels, and Beyond* (New York: First Second, 2008).

Collaborative Art

Keith Knight and Mat Schwarzman, *Beginner's Guide to Community-Based Arts* (Oakland, CA: New Village Press. 2005).

Marit Dewhurst, "Where are we? Mapping the field of community arts," *International Journal of Education Through Art* 8, no. 3 (2012): 321–328, doi: io.i386/eta.8.3.32i_7.

Notes

DEDICATION

1. Richard Elman, "A Rap On Race," *New York Times*, June 27, 1971, http://www.nytimes.com/
books/98/03/29/specials/baldwin-race.html.

FOREWORD

1. See quote from Alex Grey at https://www.healing-power-of-art.org/benefits-of-art/.

PREFACE

1. Gloria Anzaldúa, *Borderlands/La Frontera: The New Mestiza* (San Francisco: Aunt Lute Books,
1987), 87.
2. Paulo Freire, *Teachers As Cultural Workers: Letters to Those Who Dare Teach* (Boulder, CO:
Westview Press, 1998), 73.
3. Gloria Anzaldúa, This Bridge *We Call Home: Radical Visions for Transformation* (New York:
Routledge, 2002), 1.

INTRODUCTION

1. "Grace Lee Boggs: A Century in the World," interview by Krista Tippet and Richard
Feldman, *On Being*, National Public Radio, August 27, 2015, https://onbeing.org/programs/
grace-lee-boggs-a-century-in-the-world/1060/.
2. According to a 2016 report by the Department of Education, 82% of elementary and secondary
teachers in public schools are white. "The State of Racial Diversity in the Educator Workforce,"
US Department of Education, July 2016, https://www2.ed.gov/rschstat/eval/highered/racial
-diversity/state-racial-diversity-workforce.pdf; "Projections of the Size and Composition of the
U.S. Population: 2014 to 2060," US Census Bureau, https://www.census.gov/content/dam
/Census/library/publications/2015/demo/p25-1143.pdf.
3. Christopher Emdin, *For White Folks Who Teach in the Hood . . . and the Rest of Y'all Too*
(Boston: Beacon Press, 2016), 19.
4. Throughout this book I use the term "students" to describe the adult participants in my course.
The majority of these students were preservice art teachers, though most had some introductory
teaching experiences in museums, community centers, or schools. Several were seasoned teachers returning to graduate school for additional certification.
5. Mark R. Warren, *Dry Bones Rattling: Community Building to Revitalize American Democracy*
(Princeton, NJ: Princeton University Press, 2001); Kimberly Bobo et al., *Organizing for Social*

Change: Midwest Academy Manual for Activists (Santa Ana, CA: Roundhouse Publishing, 2001); Paul J. Kuttner, "Educating for cultural citizenship: Reframing the goals of arts education," *Curriculum Inquiry* 45 (2015): 69–92, doi: 10.1080/03626784.2014.980940.

6. Barbara Kirshenblatt-Gimblett, "An Accessible Aesthetic: The Role of Folk Arts and the Folk Artist in the Curriculum," *New York Folklore: The Journal of the New York Folklore Society* 9 (1983): 9–18; Marsha MacDowell, ed., *Folk Arts In Education: A Resource Handbook* (East Lansing: Michigan State University, 1987); Paddy Bowman, "'Oh, That's Just Folklore': Valuing the Ordinary as an Extraordinary Teaching Tool," in *Language Arts* 81(2004): 385–95.

7. Kirshenblatt-Gimblett, "An Accessible Aesthetic."

8. Sonia Nieto and Patty Bode, *Affirming Diversity: The Sociopolitical Context of Multicultural Education* (Boston: University of Massachusetts, 2011); Christine E. Sleeter and Carl A. Grant, *Making Choices for Multicultural Education: Five approaches to race, class, and gender* (UK: Wiley, 2008); Geneva Gay and James Banks, "Culturally Responsive Teaching: Theory, Research, and Practice," in *Multicultural Education Series* 8 (New York: Teachers' College Press, 2000).

9. Ana María Villegas and Tamara Lucas, "Preparing Culturally Responsive Teachers: Rethinking the Curriculum," *Journal of Teacher Education* 53 (2002): 20–32.

10. Dipti Desai, Jessica Hamlin, and Rachel Mattson, *History as Art, Art as History: Contemporary Art and Social Studies Education* (New York: Routledge, 2009); Marit Dewhurst, *Social Justice Art: A Framework for Activist Art Pedagogy* (Cambridge, MA: Harvard Educational Publishing Group, 2014); Therese Quinn, John Ploof, and Lisa Hochtritt, ed., *Art and Social Justice Education: Culture as Commons* (New York: Routledge, 2011).

11. Canadian AIDS Treatment Information Exchange, *Empower: Youth, Arts, and Activism. An HIV/AIDS Arts Activism Manual for Youth by Youth* (Toronto: Centre for Urban Health Initiatives), http://www.catie.ca/sites/default/files/empower-youthartsandactivism%20.pdf.

12. Graeme Chalmers, *Celebrating Pluralism: Art, Education, and Cultural Diversity* (Santa Monica, CA: Getty Education Institute for the Arts, 1996); Elliot W. Eisner, *The Arts and the Creation of Mind* (New Haven, CT: Yale University Press, 2002); June King McFee, *Cultural Diversity and the Structure and Practice of Art Education* (Reston, VA: The National Art Education Association, 1998).

13. Chalmers, *Celebrating Pluralism*, 26.

14. Nina Felshin, ed., *But Is It Art? The Spirit of Art as Activism* (Seattle, WA: Bay Press, 1995); Lucy R. Lippard, *Mixed Blessings: New Art in a Multicultural America* (New York: Pantheon Books, 1990); T. V. Reed, *The Art of Protest: Culture and Activism from the Civil Rights Movement to the Streets of Seattle* (Minneapolis: University of Minnesota Press, 2005); Nicolas Lampert, *A People's Art History of the United States 250 Years of Activist Art and Artists Working in Social Justice Movements* (New York: New Press, 2015).

15. Susan Cahan and Zoya Kocur, *Contemporary Art and Multicultural Education* (New York: Routledge 1999), 141.

16. Baldwin, "The Creative Process."

17. We spend significant time in class discussing the concept of "community." Here, and throughout this book, I use it to describe a group of people who share some common identity. As students reflect on their experience throughout the course, we discuss questions about how and by whom communities are formed, what forces determine membership in communities, insider and outsider status, and how communities evolve and shift based on factors of power, privilege, ownership, time, and location.

18. Like any empirical study, there are certainly limitations to this research. The small sample size of participants drawn from former students means that the findings of this study are based on a limited number of responses. In addition, as both their former professor and the principal

investigator of the study, there is the chance that participants' responses may be colored by our personal and professional relationships. To the best of my ability, I have tried to mitigate this bias, but these overlapping roles nevertheless affect any research. It is also important to note that the course on which the research is based takes place at a very particular moment in time in a very specific learning environment. While I believe the findings from this work are applicable in other settings and with other audiences, the art education program at City College tends to attract students who are interested in learning about identity, justice, and community organizing as it relates to the arts. Students know that in accepting their place in the program, they will be required and expected to engage in conversations about social and cultural identity, systemic oppression, culturally relevant pedagogy, and community building through the arts. Furthermore, as one of the nation's most ethnically diverse student bodies, City College courses tend to be filled with populations that are more racially, culturally, economically, and nationally diverse than the majority of comparable graduate and undergraduate education programs across the country. Because of this, the class discussions we engage in often include a rich range of perspectives and experiences that support the practice of cross-cultural communication. Educators who aim to translate the findings from this study to other settings will need to attend to the unique characteristics of their own contexts by adjusting the activities using some of the strategies I will highlight through the book.

19. Joseph Weixlmann, *Black Feminist Criticism and Critical Theory* (Michigan: Penkevill Publishing Company, 1988), 200.
20. Emdin, *For White Folks Who Teach in the Hood*, 43.
21. Jeff Chang, *We Gon' Be Alright* (New York: Picador, 2016), 165.

CHAPTER 1

1. Gloria E. Anzaldúa, preface, *This Bridge We Call Home: Radical Visions for Transformation* (New York: Routledge, 2002), 3.
2. Audre Lorde, "Age, Race, Class and Sex: Women Redefining Difference," in *Sister Outsider: Essays and Speeches* (Freedom, CA: Crossing Press, 1984), 115.
3. Ibid.
4. Gwyn Kirk and Margo Ōkazawa-Rey, "Identities and Social Location: Who Am I? Who Are My People?," in *Readings for Diversity and Social Justice*, ed. Maurianne Adams et al. (New York: Routledge, 2010), 8.
5. Ibid., 12.
6. Ibid.
7. Ibid., 13.
8. Ibid.
9. bell hooks, "Eating the Other: Desire and Resistance," in *Black Looks: Race and Representation* (Boston: South End Press, 1992), 21.
10. Ibid., 39.
11. Ibid., 24.
12. Ibid., 28.
13. Ibid.
14. Lisa Delpit, *Other People's Children: Cultural Conflict in the Classroom* (New York: The New Press, 2006), 47.
15. Brian Arao and Kristi Clemens, "From Safe Spaces to Brave Spaces: A New Way to Frame Dialogue Around Diversity and Social Justice," in *The Art of Effective Facilitation: Reflections from Social Justice Educators*, ed. Lisa Landreman (Sterling, VA: Stylus Publishing, 2013), 135–50.

16. Leigh Patel, "Pedagogies of Resistance and Survivance: Learning as Marronage," *Equity and Excellence in Education* 49 (2016): 397, doi: 10.1080/10665684.2016.1227585.
17. Edward Curtis, *The North American Indian* (Cambridge, MA: The University Press, 1907–30).
18. Lucy R. Lippard, "Around Here," in *The Lure of the Local: Senses of Place in a Multicentered Society* (New York: New Press, 1997), 24.
19. Delpit, *Other People's Children*, 47.
20. Desmond Tutu, *No Future Without Forgiveness* (New York: Random House, 2000), 31.
21. Ibid.

CHAPTER 2

1. President Barack Obama and Marilynne Robinson, "President Obama & Marilynne Robinson: A Conversation—II," *New York Book Review*, November 19, 2015, http://www.nybooks.com /articles/2015/11/19/president-obama-marilynne-robinson-conversation-2/.
2. Ralph Ellison, *Invisible Man* (New York: Vintage International, 1995), 3.
3. William Ayers, *To Teach: The Journey of a Teacher* (New York: Teachers College Press, 2001), 25; bell hooks, *Teaching to Transgress: Education as the Practice of Freedom* (New York: Routledge, 1994); Lisa Delpit, *Other People's Children: Cultural Conflict in the Classroom* (New York: New Press, 2006); Christopher Emdin, *For White Folks Who Teach in the Hood . . . and the Rest of Ya'll Too* (Boston: Beacon Press, 2014).
4. Ayers, *To Teach: The Journey of a Teacher.*
5. Paddy Bowman, "'Oh, That's Just Folklore': Valuing the Ordinary as an Extraordinary Teaching Tool," *Language Arts* 81 (2004): 385–95; Susan Eleuterio, Andrea Graham, Gail Mathews-DeNatale, and Rachelle Saltzman, "How Community Can be Understood and Studied Through Ethnic Contributions" (essays presented at the 1997 Iowa Folklife Education Seminar, Iowa, 1997); Sonia Nieto, *The Light in Their Eyes: Creating Multicultural Learning Communities*, ed. James A. Bank (New York: Teachers College Press, 2010); Wayne Au, *Rethinking Multicultural Education: Teaching for Racial and Cultural Justice* (Milwaukee, WI: Rethinking Schools Ltd., 2009); Enid Lee, Deborah Menkart, and Margo Ōkazawa-Rey, *Beyond Heroes and Holidays* (Washington, DC: Teaching For Change, 2011).
6. Jeff Chang, *We Gon' Be Alright* (New York: Picador, 2016), 167.
7. Joshua Aronson, "Knowing Students as Individuals," in *Everyday Antiracism: Getting Real About Race in School*, ed. Mica Pollock (New York: New Press, 2008), 67.
8. Gwyn Kirk and Margo Ōkazawa-Rey, "Identities and Social Location: Who Am I? Who Are My People?," in *Readings for Diversity and Social Justice*, ed. Maurianne Adams et al. (New York: Routledge, 2010); Robin DiAngelo and Özlem Sensoy, *Is Everyone Really Equal?*, ed. James A. Bank (New York: Teachers College Press, 2017).
9. Ana María Villegas and Tamara Lucas, "Preparing Culturally Responsive Teachers: Rethinking thecurriculum,"*JournalofTeacherEducation*53(2002):20–32,doi:10.1177/0022487102053001003; Geneva Gay, *Culturally Responsive Teaching: Theory, Practice, & Research* (New York: Teachers College Press, 2000); Au, *Rethinking Multicultural Education*; Nieto, *The Light in Their Eyes.*
10. Lucy R. Lippard, "Around Here," in *The Lure of the Local: Senses of Place in a Multicentered Society* (New York: New Press, 1997), 24; Kimberly Powell, "Viewing Places: Students as Visual Ethnographers," *Art Education* 44 (2010): 44–53; Maxine Greene, *Releasing The Imagination: Essays on Education, the Arts, and Social Change* (San Francisco: Jossey-Bass Publishers, 1995).
11. JR, "Women Are Heroes," http://www.jr-art.net/projects/women-are-heroes-brazil.
12. From protocols and pedagogical approaches such as Abigail Housen and Philip Yenawine's Visual Thinking Strategies to Project Zero's Visible Thinking Routines, and Rika Burnham and Elliot Kai-Kee's discussion of extended guided looking, there are many resources for facilitating

conversations about works of art. Whether viewed as techniques to develop visual literacy, as tools to teach art history, or as opportunities to support critical thinking, the task of looking closely at a work of art and engaging in discussion with others can provide important possibilities to talk about identity, difference, and the relationships between people. "About Us," Visual Thinking Strategies, https://vtshome.org/about/; "Visual Thinking," Project Zero, http://www .pz.harvard.edu/projects/visible-thinking; Rika Burnham, *Teaching in the Art Museum: Interpretation as Experience* (Los Angeles: Getty Publications, 2011).

13. For example, to teach about kente cloth, you might share connections not just to black or African history, but also to the traditions of textile production in other regions of the world. You might encourage students to explore how the patterns of kente cloth exist in our contemporary visual environment and how the messages and stories conveyed by these patterns have shifted over time and place. You might look to people who have worn kente cloth throughout history to analyze how the textile has played different roles for different people. You might even use this as a moment to talk about what happens when people from outside the original West African traditions wear or use kente cloth. You might research contemporary kente cloth production and compare it to the handwoven techniques of older examples, perhaps assessing how politics, economics, and even environmental factors have shaped access to modes and materials of kente cloth production.

14. For additional suggestions on formulating inquiry questions, see the work of Abigail Housen and Philip Yenawine, Rika Turnham and Elliot Kai-Kee, and the regular features on artmuseumteaching.com.

15. Susan Sontag, *On Photography* (New York: Farrar, Straus and Giroux, 1977), 14.

16. "Lalla Essaydi," Edwynn Houk Gallery, http://www.houkgallery.com/artists/lalla-essaydi?view =slider.

CHAPTER 3

1. Hilary Holladay, *Wild Blessings: The Poetry of Lucille Clifton* (Baton Rouge, LA: LSU Press, 2004), 194.

2. Maxine Greene, *Releasing the Imagination: Essays on Education, the Arts, and Social Change* (San Francisco: Jossey-Bass Publishers, 1995), 11.

3. Joshua Aronson, "Knowing Students as Individuals," in *Everyday Antiracism: Getting Real About Race in School*, ed. Mica Pollock et al. (New York: New Press, 2008), 68.

4. Dipti Desai, Jessica Hamlin, and Rachel Mattson, *Constructing Race. History as Art, Art as History* (New York: Routledge, 2010), 14795; Sheng Kuan Chung, "Media Literacy Art Education: Deconstructing Lesbian and Gay Stereotypes in the Media," International Journal of Art & Design Education 26 (2007): 98–107, doi:10.1111/j.1476-8070.2007.00514; Karen Keifer-Boyd, Patricia M. Amburgy, and Wanda B. Knight, "Unpacking Privilege: Memory, Culture, Gender, Race, and Power in Visual Culture," *Art Education* 60 (2007): 19–24.

5. Lucy R. Lippard, "Around Here," in *The Lure of the Local: Senses of Place in a Multicentered Society* (New York: New Press, 1997), 22–31; Grant Kashatok and Leisy Wyman, "Getting to Know Students' Communities," in *Everyday Antiracism: Getting Real About Race in School*, ed. Mica Pollock (New York: New Press, 2008), 300.

6. Kimberly Powell, "Viewing Places: Students as Visual Ethnographers," *Art Education* 44 (2010): 44–53; Barbara Kirshenblatt-Gimblett, "An Accessible Aesthetic: The Role of Folk Arts and the Folk Artist in the Curriculum," *New York Folklore: The Journal of the New York Folklore Society* 9 (1983): 9–18; Marsha MacDowell, ed., *Folk Arts In Education: A Resource Handbook* (East Lansing: Michigan State University, 1987); Paddy Bowman, "'Oh, That's Just Folklore': Valuing the Ordinary as an Extraordinary Teaching Tool," *Language Arts* 81 (2004): 385–95.

7. Wendy Ewald, *American Alphabets*, http://wendyewald.com/portfolio/american-alphabets/.

8. Greene, *Releasing the Imagination*, 26.

9. Candy Chang, *I Wish This Was*, http://candychang.com/work/i-wish-this-was/.

10. Scott McCloud, *Understanding Comics* (New York: Kitchen Sink Press, 1993), 36.

11. S. Bey, "Story Drawings: Revisiting Personal Struggles, Empathizing with 'Others,'" in *Art and Social Justice Education: Culture as Commons*, ed. Lisa J. Hochtritt et al. (New York: Routledge, 2012), 136–141.

12. Lisa Delpit, "The Silenced Dialogue: Power and Pedagogy in Educating Other People's Children," *Harvard Educational Review* 58 (1988): 280–98.

13. Depending on the group, sometimes I have provided a list of potential scenarios that students can choose to illustrate. Previous scenario examples include the following: (1) a student in one of your art classes wears gender nonconforming clothes and uses they/them as their preferred pronouns. Other students and a few of the faculty describe this student as gay though the student has never said anything to you; (2) last night you just organized the first exhibition of student artwork at your school. Turnout was low; a fellow teacher tries to console you by saying, "Well, you know, don't expect too much—their parents just don't care."

14. Beverly Tatum, *Why Are All the Black Kids Sitting Together in the Cafeteria* (New York: Basic Books), 200.

15. Aronson, "Knowing Students as Individuals," 68.

16. Delpit, "The Silenced Dialogue," 297.

17. A note on empathy: as educator and scholar Leigh Patel reminds us, "Empathy does not require realignment of social relations. This is not to say that it cannot be a component of social transformation," but without a critical analysis of how power affects our relationships, empathy can quickly slip into a kind of patronizing sympathy or pity that can deepen our assumptions and perpetuate inequality. Leigh Patel, "The Irrationality of Anti-Racist Empathy," *The English Journal* 106, No. 2. (2016): 81–84.

CHAPTER 4

1. bell hooks, *Teaching Community: A Pedagogy of Hope* (New York: Routledge, 2003), 197.

2. Reading scholar Eve Tuck's work, I'm reminded that even in naming the stereotypes, we give them dangerous breathing room. As Tuck writes, "[W]e arrive at a paradox of damage: to refute it, we need to say it aloud." However, I include these here because I believe that they will remind many readers of their own stereotypes and hope that in seeing their ideas here, they can see why we must work against them. Eve Tuck, "Suspending Damage: A Letter to Communities," *Harvard Educational Review* 79, no. 2 (2009): 417.

3. "Indian Jewelry Lesson Plan," DickBlick, https://www.dickblick.com/multicultural/indian jewelry/.

4. Sarah B. Shear, Ryan T. Knowles, Gregory J. Soden, and Antonio J. Castro, "Manifesting Destiny: Re/presentations of Indigenous Peoples in K–12 U.S. History Standards," *Theory & Research in Social Education* 43 (2015): 68–101, doi: 10.1080/00933104.2014.999849.

5. Zora Neale Hurston, *Dust Tracks on a Road* (New York: Harper Collins, 2006), 143.

6. Tuck, "Suspending Damage," 416.

7. See Eve Tuck's work on "repatriation" in research for an eloquent proposal of how scholars can reimagine their work. Eve Tuck, "Rematriating Curriculum Studies," *Journal of Curriculum & Pedagogy* 8, no. 1 (2011): 34–37.

8. Mark Addison Smith, "Project Research" (syllabus, City College of New York, New York, 2016).

9. John Paul Rangel, "Indigenous Perspectives on Contemporary Native Art, Indigenous Aesthetics and Representation" (PhD diss., University of New Mexico, 2013).

10. Ibid.

11. Ibid.

12. "Brian Jungen: Crafting Everyday Objects into Art," *All Things Considered*, NPR, https://www.npr.org/templates/story/story.php?storyId=113840238.

13. Hương Ngô (artist), email message to author, July 16, 2017.

14. Chimamanda Ngozi Adichie, "The danger of a single story," TEDGlobal 2009, https://www.ted.com/talks/chimamanda_adichie_the_danger_of_a_single_story.

15. Tuck, "Suspending Damage," 416.

16. Howard Zinn, *A People's History of the United States: 1942–Present* (New York: Routledge, 2013), 683.

17. Tuhiwai Smith's *Decolonizing Methodologies* challenges educators and researchers to rethink conventional paradigms of time, space, and research. Linda Tuhiwai Smith, *Decolonizing Methodologies* (New York: Zed Books, 1999).

18. Lisa (Leigh) Patel, *Youth Held at the Border: Immigration, Education, and the Politics of Inclusion* (New York: Teachers College Press, 2013), 36.

19. Tuhiwai Smith, *Decolonizing Methodologies*, 34.

CHAPTER 5

1. bell hooks, *All About Love: New Visions* (New York: William Morrow, 2000), 93.

2. bell hooks, *Teaching to Transgress* (New York: Routledge, 1994), 8.

3. Elisabeth Soep, "Youth Mediate Democracy," *National Civic Review* 95 (2006): 34–40, doi: 10.1002/ncr.129.

4. Paulo Freire, *Pedagogy of the Oppressed* (New York: Continuum Press, 1970); hooks, *Teaching to Transgress*; William Ayers and Ryan Alexander-Tanner, "Liberating the Curriculum," in *To Teach: the journey, in comics* (New York: Teachers College Press, 2010), 67–80; Korina Jocson and Brett Cook, "Pedagogy, Collaboration, and Transformation: A conversation with Brett Cook," in *Art and Social Justice Education: Culture as Commons*, ed. Therese M. Quinn et al. (New York: Routledge, 2011) 89–94.

5. Alice Walker, *We Are the Ones We Have Been Waiting For* (New York: New York Press, 2006), 141.

6. Lynda Barry, *Syllabus: Notes from an Accidental Professor* (Montreal: Drawn & Quarterly, 2014).

7. Puerto Rican water bread.

8. bell hooks, *Teaching Community: A Pedagogy of Hope* (New York: Routledge, 2003), 36.

9. Sonia Sanchez, "Ruminations/Reflections (1984)," in *I'm Black When I'm Singing, I'm Blue When I Ain't and Other Plays*, ed. Jacqueline Wood (Durham, NC: Duke University Press, 2010), 15.

10. Ibid., 15.

11. "Inquiry and Action: Arzu Mistry's 'Unfolding Practice,'" Women's Studio Workshop, http://www.wsworkshop.org/2016/06/arzu-mistry/.

12. Gloria Anzaldúa, *Borderlands/La Frontera: The New Mestiza* (San Francisco: Aunt Lute Books, 1987), 87.

13. *Podcast #47: Ntozake Shange on Inspiration and Harlem*, NYPL (podcast), https://www.nypl.org/blog/2015/02/06/podcast-ntozake-shange.

CHAPTER 6

1. Toni Morrison, "No Place for Self-Pity, No Room for Fear," *The Nation*, March 23, 2015, https://www.thenation.com/article/no-place-self-pity-no-room-fear/.

2. As two celebrated and controversial musicals, both *The King and I* and *South Pacific* challenged and perpetuated stereotypes of the day. Their portrayals of Southeast Asians and Pacific Islanders are deeply offensive and flawed, just as their depictions of whites are glorified. For now, I include both here as reminders of the often contradictory messages we receive about identity, and as a nod to my grandmother.

3. Christopher Emdin, *For White Folks Who Teach in the Hood . . . and the Rest of Ya'll Too* (Boston: Beacon Press, 2014).

ACKNOWLEDGMENTS

1. bell hooks, *All About Love: New Visions* (New York: William Morrow, 2000), 93.

2. James Baldwin, "The Creative Process," in *Creative America* (New York: Ridge Press, 1962).

3. Assata Shakur, "Affirmation," in *Assata: An Autobiography* (Chicago: Lawrence Hill Books, 1987/2001), 1.

4. Gloria Anzaldúa, "Foreword to the Second Edition, 1983," in *This Bridge Called My Back* (Albany, NY: SUNY Press, 2015), 254.

5. Sherman Alexie, "Hymn," *Early Bird Books*, last modified August 16, 2017, https://earlybirdbooks .com/hymn-a-new-poem-by-sherman-alexie.

Acknowledgments

O n days when the writing is slow, my teaching feels muddled, and the world seems to be crumbling, I think of the graciousness and courage of the artist-educator-students with whom I have the true honor of working. As they juggle the many complications of life and graduate school in their quest to be outstanding arts educators in urban schools and museums, they maintain a constant focus of purpose—to be the kinds of educators who value, uplift, and challenge young people to be critical agents of creative change. Despite the many obstacles to teaching today and the rising tides of inequality in our society, these students consistently choose to love the young people they work with and the possibilities they embody. As they do, they remind me of the words of bell hooks that I quote in this book, who writes, "When we choose to love, we choose to move against fear, against alienation and separation. The choice to love is a choice to connect, to find ourselves in the other."[1] Teaching and learning with artist-educators who seek to move beyond their own fears to see our shared humanity has been one of my greatest joys. This book exists because of these artist-educator-students; I am indebted to each of them. Through our candid and difficult conversations about the socially constructed walls that divide us, the students I have worked with have taught me much about the importance of vulnerability, hope, and imagination. While every student who has taken my course has contributed in some way to the thinking behind this book, several were generous enough to spend additional time talking with me at length about their reflections. Thank you, Max Allbee, Jackie Du, Jasmin Eli-Washington, Rosalinda Glennon, Will Goertzel, Kendra Grady, Olivia Kalin, Stefanie Lewin, Rafaela Luna, Shannon Murphy, Natalie Nieves, Chris Parkman, Leena Peter-Uitto, Margaret Phelan, Avery Powell, Elle Sauer, Roberto Soto, Kendra Torres, Rafael Vélez Jr., Andy Vernon-Jones, Jose-Manuel

Villeneuve, Katie Walters, and Alexandra Whedbee. Their eloquent thoughts are the foundation of this book. I have additional gratitude for students who kindly allowed me to write about their artwork: Florence Gidez, Jack Gomez, Charles Kushla, Lissette Pardo, Christopher Rose, Benjamin Russell, Jarin Tasnem, and Jocelyn Hsin-ju Yang.

Writing a book about how we can try to nurture relationships across the lines of difference we are taught to believe in has been challenging in that it demanded that I too embrace the kind of vulnerability and introspection into my own biases that I ask of my students. Along the way, several educator-scholars whom I am lucky to call dear friends have read sections and provided much-needed feedback and encouragement. In moments when I was ready to quit, their clarity and faith in this book reminded me of the words of James Baldwin when he writes: "The precise role of the artist, then, is to illuminate that darkness, blaze roads through that vast forest, so that we will not, in all our doing, lose sight of its purpose, which is, after all, to make the world a more human dwelling place."[2] Thank you, Keonna Hendrick, Malia Villegas, Amy Kraehe, Anika Selhorst, and Yabome Kabia Casper for helping me maintain the hope, criticality, and vulnerability necessary to keep writing, and for the ways in which you each work every day to make this world more humane.

I am deeply grateful to the team who supported the production of this book. I appreciate the nimble-fingered transcribers who worked with ever-increasing numbers of interviews: Gina Luz Abood, Sue Mason, Ameerah Saidi, and Amanda Sensel. I am thankful for Eileen Emond's speedy citations and inspiring artist research. The team of editors, production managers, and marketing folks at the Harvard Education Press have made publishing a book seem simple, something it certainly is not. Their precision processes are matched only by their kindness. Throughout the development of this book, Nancy Walser, my editor-turned-comrade, has offered me critical feedback, endless encouragement, and a vision for how this book may be useful for the field.

My cheering section of friends and family—many of whom are also gifted educators themselves—have helped turn this book from idea into actual pages through their consistent care, gentle nudging, provocative questioning, and endless patience. Activist Assata Shakur writes "I believe in the sweat of love/and in the fire of truth./And I believe that a lost ship,/ steered by tired, seasick sailors,/ can still be guided home to port."[3] For your tireless belief, guidance, and love, thank you, Sarah Miner, Marcella Runnell Hall, Keisha

Green, Lucie Morel, Diana Trautner Smith, Chantal Francois, Michael Kieffer, Elvedin Lukovic, Radhika Rao, Vajra Watson, Shari Katz Graham, Lonnie Firestone, Raygine D'Aquoi, Lauren Barkan, Susan McCullough, Heather Maxson, Ivelys Figueroa, Maya Valladares, Carla Repice, Kiran Chandra, Priyanka Dasgupta, Abby Kornfeld, Maria Politarhos, Edwin Lamboy, Clare Luz, April Burko, Gloria Sensel, Jean Kroeber, and Samara Hoyer-Winfield. I am ever grateful to my parents, Marsha MacDowell and Kurt Dewhurst, for their love and for embodying Gloria Anzaldúa's words: "*Caminante, no hay puentes, se hace puentes al andar.* (Voyager, there are no bridges, one builds them as one walks.)"[4] And to Nathan Sensel and Desi Sensel-Dewhurst for not letting me quit, for understanding the many hours away from you both, and for believing that a better world is possible—thank you forever. Let us keep committing ourselves to the beautiful struggle and, as Sherman Alexie writes, "We will be courageous with our love. We will risk danger/ As we sing and sing and sing to welcome strangers."[5]

About the Author

Marit Dewhurst is the director of art education and associate professor in art and museum education at the City College of New York (CCNY). She has worked as an educator and program coordinator in multiple settings both nationally and abroad, including community centers, museums, juvenile detention centers, and international development projects. Building on her work in museums, she collaborated with youth activists to develop Museum Teen Summit, a youth-led research and advocacy program for museum teen programs. Since 2013, she has facilitated multiple workshops with youth, educators, and artists on the role of art education in teaching about the Movement for Black Lives. Working with educator Keonna Hendrick, she has also co-led professional development sessions across the country, focusing on cultural equity and inclusion in museums and other arts organizations. Her research and teaching interests include community organizing, antiracist education, museum and art education, and how young people, artists, and educators play key roles in justice-oriented social change. Publications include chapters in several books on art in social justice education and antiracist museum education as well as articles in *Equity & Excellence in Education, The Journal of Museum Education, The Journal of Art Education, International Journal of Education through Art*, and *Harvard Educational Review*. Her book, *Social Justice Art: A Framework for Activist Art Pedagogy* is used in classrooms, museums, and teacher-training programs in the United States and abroad.

Index